Basic

BROCHURES

BASIC BROCHURES

INDEX BOOK, SL
Consell de Cent, 160 local 3
08015 Barcelona
T +34 93 454 5547
F +34 93 454 8438
ib@indexbook.com
www.indexbook.com

Publisher: Sylvie Estrada
Design: Ivana Kábelová
ISBN: 978-84-92643-73-8

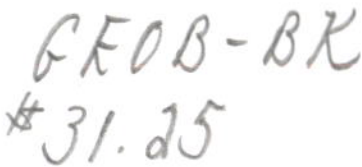

Basic BROCHURES

Pages

No Fold
Single Fold
Multiple Folds
Final Directory

No Fold

008 - 029

001/
Anna Farré / LILA&TOM • *Children's Fashion Collection 2010-2011 for La Compagnie des Petits*

002/
Beatriz Gimeno Sanz • *Information leaflets for a centre offering social services to families experiencing separation and divorce*

003/
Anna Pigem, photographer Elisabet Serra • *Pamphlet for Biennal 2008, the 5th biennial art exhibition sponsored by Casa de Cultura de la Diputació de Girona*

004/
Cubo Diseño • *Folder and inserts for Construcciones y Auxiliar de Ferrocarriles (CAF) annual report on occupational health and safety*

005/
Manuel Gracia Gascón • *Developed piece for collection showcase, to distributors and buyers*

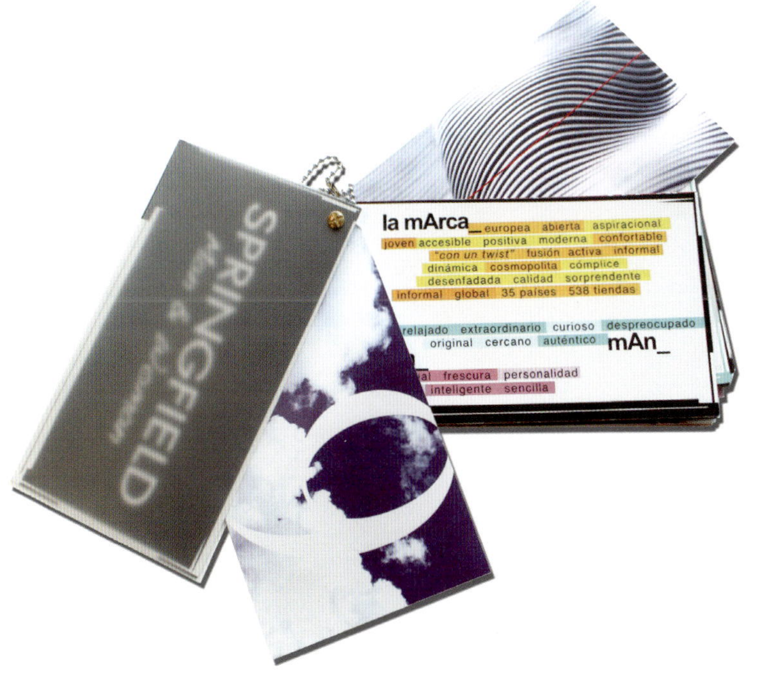
SPRINGFIELD
la mArca_
europea abierta aspiracional
joven accesible positiva moderna confortable
"con un twist" fusión activa informal
dinámica cosmopolita cómplice
desenfadada calidad sorprendente
informal global 35 países 538 tiendas
relajado extraordinario curioso despreocupado
original cercano auténtico mAn_
frescura personalidad
inteligente sencilla

No Fold

SPRINGFIELD
SPRINGFIELD

006/
Mora Azul Estudio • *Folder and inserts promoting the concept, design, layout and presentation of Minimalistic Pavilions, an upscale housing complex*

007/
Nifava • *Ballot-style invitations encouraging participation in a contest for La Mostra de Pessebres d'Olot*

CONCURS
D'IDEES

008/
oikos associati • *Folder and thematic brochures for Tearose, an Italy-based purveyor of luxury goods and services*

tearose
tearose
tearose
tearose
tearose

tearose wedding concierge®
tearose

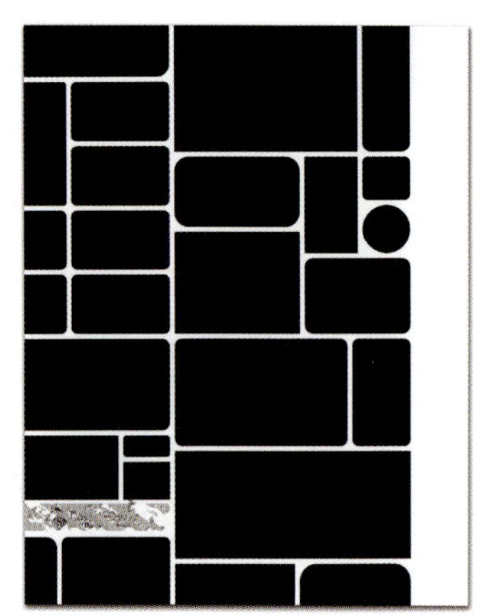

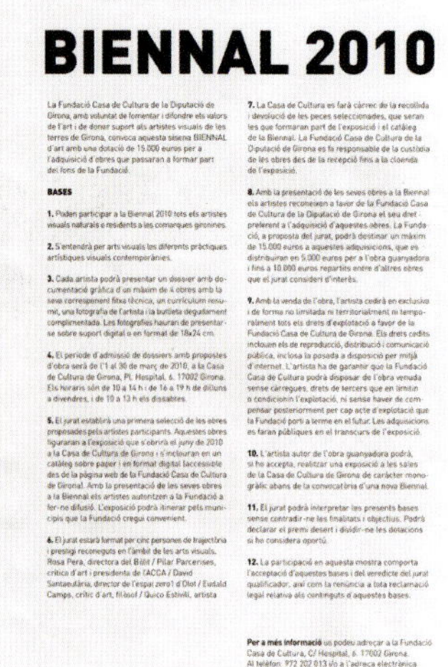

BIENNAL 2010

La Fundació Casa de Cultura de la Diputació de Girona, amb voluntat de fomentar i difondre els valors de l'art i de donar suport als artistes visuals de les terres de Girona, convoca aquesta sisena BIENNAL d'art amb una dotació de 15.000 euros per a l'adquisició d'obres que passaran a formar part del fons de la Fundació.

BASES

1. Poden participar a la Biennal 2010 tots els artistes visuals naturals o residents a les comarques gironines.

2. S'entendrà per arts visuals les diferents pràctiques artístiques visuals contemporànies.

3. Cada artista podrà presentar un dossier amb documentació gràfica d'un màxim de 4 obres amb la seva corresponent fitxa tècnica, un currículum resumit, una fotografia de l'artista i la butlleta degudament complimentada. Les fotografies hauran de presentar-se sobre suport digital o en format de 18x24 cm.

4. El període d'admissió de dossiers amb propostes d'obra serà de l'1 al 30 de març de 2010, a la Casa de Cultura de Girona, Pl. Hospital, 6. 17002 Girona. Els horaris són de 10 a 14 h i de 16 a 19 h de dilluns a divendres, i de 10 a 13 h els dissabtes.

5. El jurat establirà una primera selecció de les obres proposades pels artistes participants. Aquestes obres figuraran a l'exposició que s'obrirà el juny de 2010 a la Casa de Cultura de Girona i s'inclouran en un catàleg sobre paper i en format digital (accessible des de la pàgina web de la Fundació Casa de Cultura de Girona). Amb la presentació de les seves obres a la Biennal els artistes autoritzen a la Fundació a fer-ne difusió. L'exposició podrà itinerar pels municipis que la Fundació cregui convenient.

6. El jurat estarà format per cinc persones de trajectòria i prestigi reconeguts en l'àmbit de les arts visuals. Rosa Pera, directora del Bòlit / Pilar Parcerisas, crítica d'art i presidenta de l'ACCA / David Santaeulària, director de l'espai zero1 d'Olot / Eudald Camps, crític d'art, filòsof / Quico Estivill, artista

7. La Casa de Cultura es farà càrrec de la recollida i devolució de les peces seleccionades, que seran les que formaran part de l'exposició i el catàleg de la Biennal. La Fundació Casa de Cultura de la Diputació de Girona es fa responsable de la custòdia de les obres des de la recepció fins a la cloenda de l'exposició.

8. Amb la presentació de les seves obres a la Biennal els artistes reconeixen a favor de la Fundació Casa de Cultura de la Diputació de Girona el seu dret preferent a l'adquisició d'aquestes obres. La Fundació, a proposta del jurat, podrà destinar un màxim de 15.000 euros a aquestes adquisicions, que es distribuiran en 5.000 euros per a l'obra guanyadora i fins a 10.000 euros repartits entre d'altres obres que el jurat consideri d'interès.

9. Amb la venda de l'obra, l'artista cedirà en exclusiva i de forma no limitada ni territorialment ni temporalment tots els drets d'explotació a favor de la Fundació Casa de Cultura de Girona. Els drets cedits inclouen els de reproducció, distribució i comunicació pública, inclosa la posada a disposició per mitjà d'internet. L'artista ha de garantir que la Fundació Casa de Cultura podrà disposar de l'obra venuda sense càrregues, drets de tercers que en limitin o condicionin l'explotació, ni sense haver de compensar posteriorment per cap acte d'explotació que la Fundació porti a terme en el futur. Les adquisicions es faran públiques en el transcurs de l'exposició.

10. L'artista autor de l'obra guanyadora podrà, si ho accepta, realitzar una exposició a les sales de la Casa de Cultura de Girona de caràcter monogràfic abans de la convocatòria d'una nova Biennal.

11. El jurat podrà interpretar les presents bases sense contradir-ne les finalitats i objectius. Podrà declarar el premi desert i dividir-ne les dotacions si ho considera oportú.

12. La participació en aquesta mostra comporta l'acceptació d'aquestes bases i del veredicte del jurat qualificador, així com la renúncia a tota reclamació legal relativa als continguts d'aquestes bases.

Per a més informació us podeu adreçar a la Fundació Casa de Cultura, C/ Hospital, 6. 17002 Girona. Al telèfon 972 202 013 i/o a l'adreça electrònica biennal@casadecultura.org

009/
Anna Pigem • *Catalogue-envelope with the instructions for visual artists who wish to participate in Biennal 2010, the 6th biennial art exhibition sponsored by Casa de Cultura de la Diputació de Girona*

010/
Fons Hickmann m23 • *Programme brochures for every opera premiere at Semperoper Dresden*

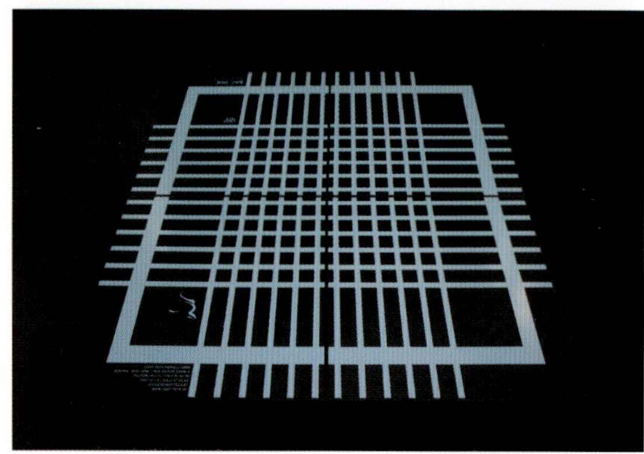

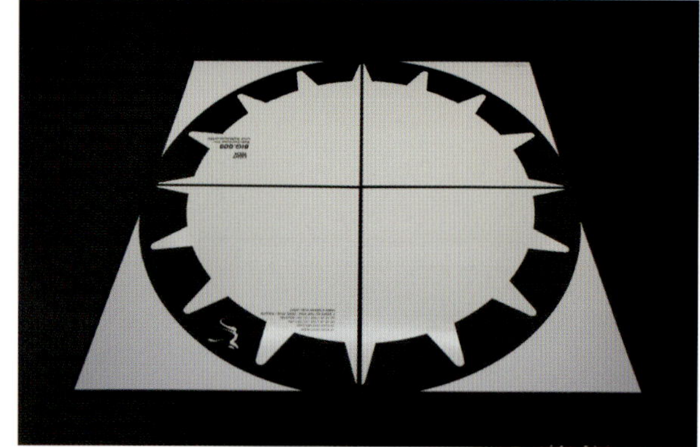

011/
Alex Grimm • *Five product folder in board game style - packaged in an individually designed slipcase*

BAC.008

LIGHT
TECH

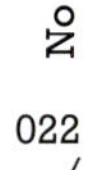
No Fold

LIGHT
TECH

012/
Konstantyner Communication & Design • *Flip-page book illustrating the functionality of NAP(TM) chairs designed by Kasper Salto*

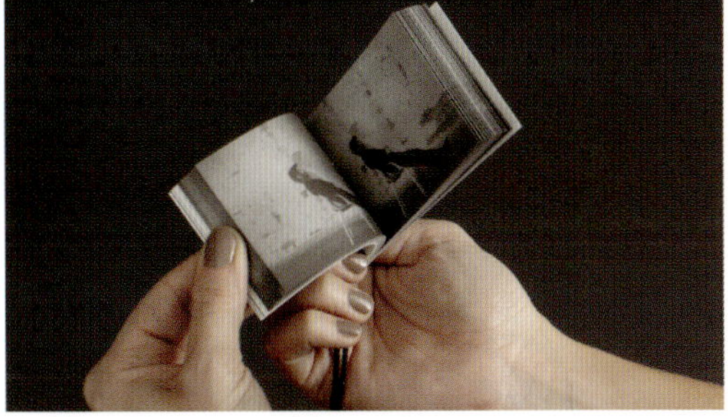

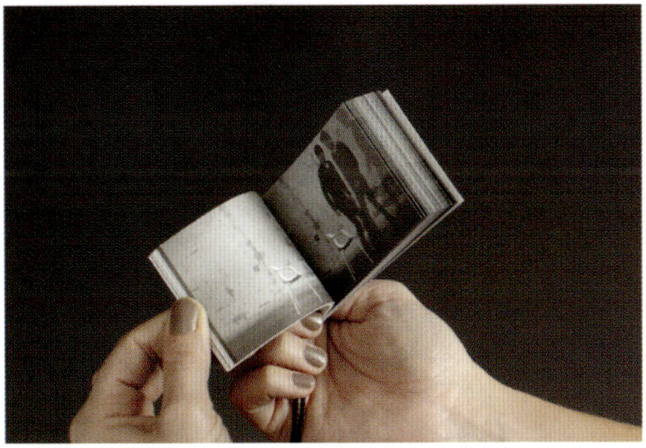

013/
Instituto de Gestión de la Información, S.L. • *Book illustrating characters found in the 3D-animated feature, Los Ladrones de Cromopolis*

001/ - Brochure number
Anna Farré / LILA&TOM - Studio name
La Compagnie des Petits - Client name
Spain - Country

Children's Fashion Collection 2010-2011
for La Compagnie des Petits - Brochure description

001/
Anna Farré / LILA&TOM
La Compagnie des Petits
Spain

Children's Fashion Collection 2010-2011 for La Compagnie des Petits

002/
Beatriz Gimeno Sanz
Caritas Diocesana Barbastro-Monzon
Spain

Information leaflets for a centre offering social services to families experiencing separation and divorce

003/
Anna Pigem, photographer Elisabet Serra
Casa de Cultura de Girona
Spain

Pamphlet for Biennal 2008, the 5th biennial art exhibition sponsored by Casa de Cultura de la Diputació de Girona

004/
Cubo Diseño
CAF
Spain

Folder and inserts for Construcciones y Auxiliar de Ferrocarriles (CAF) annual report on occupational health and safety

005/
Manuel Gracia Gascón
SPRINGFIELD
Spain

Developed piece for collection showcase, to distributors and buyers

006/
Mora Azul Estudio
Minimalistic Pavilions
México

Folder and inserts promoting the concept, design, layout and presentation of Minimalistic Pavilions, an upscale housing complex

007/
Nifava
Mostra de Pessebres a Olot i Museu dels Sants d'Olot
Spain

Ballot-style invitations encouraging participation in a contest for La Mostra de Pessebres d'Olot.

008/
oikos associati
tearose
Italy

Folder and thematic brochures for Tearose, an Italy-based purveyor of luxury goods and services

009/
Anna Pigem
Casa de Cultura de Girona
Spain

Cataloguet - envelope with the instructions for visual artists who wish to participate in Biennal 2010, the 6th biennial art exhibition sponsored by Casa de Cultura de la Diputació de Girona

010/
Fons Hickmann m23
Semperoper Dresden
Germany

Programme brochures for every opera premiere at Semperoper Dresden

011/
Alex Grimm
LIGHT-TECH GmbH
Austria

Five product folder in board game style - packaged in an individually designed slipcase

012/
Konstantyner Communication & Design
REPUBLIC OF Fritz Hansen
Denmark

Flip-page book illustrating the functionality of NAP(TM) chairs designed by Kasper Salto

013/
Instituto de Gestión de la Información, S.L.
AULA MOTION
Spain

Book illustrating characters found in the 3D-animated feature, Los Ladrones de Cromopolis

Single Fold

030 - 185

014/
Fons Hickmann m23 • *Exhibition brochure for Grafic Europe*

NEW YORK
Berlin

A Practice for everyday life
ART INSPECTOR

Underware
Read naked

Frédéric Teschner
DES ECOLES D'ART

015/
BURO-GDS • *I AM YOU, a book by Ellen Zhao, examines the relationship between the book and the reader*

YOU
STAND
RY?
YOU ARE
NOT
A BOOK
YOU ARE
NOT
WORDS
YOU ARE
NOT
A PHOTO

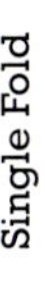

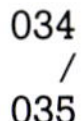

016/
MusaWorkLab • *Brochure presenting the corporate values of Centrocar in a very contemporary way*

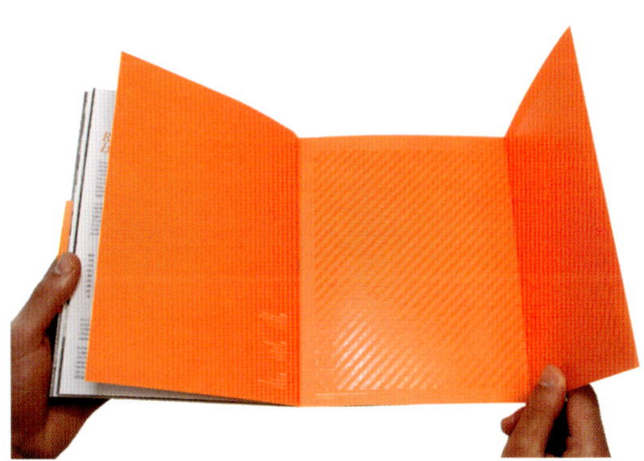

FUTURO
DE LIDERAZGO
BIENVENIDO
A CENTROCAR

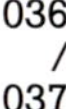

017/
ATIPUS • *Celler el Masroig winery catalogue, which incorporates product sheets that can be removed and inserted*

Solà Fred
"Negre jove de gran
intensitat colorant.
Molt aromàtic, flexible,
amb gust de fruites
madures. En boca és
fresc, amb volum,
molt equilibrat,
amb un post-gust llarg"
SOLÀ FRED

Solà Fred
"Negre jove de gran
intensitat colorant.
Molt aromàtic, flexible,
amb gust de fruites
madures. En boca és
fresc, amb volum,
molt equilibrat,
amb un post-gust llarg"
SOLÀ FRED

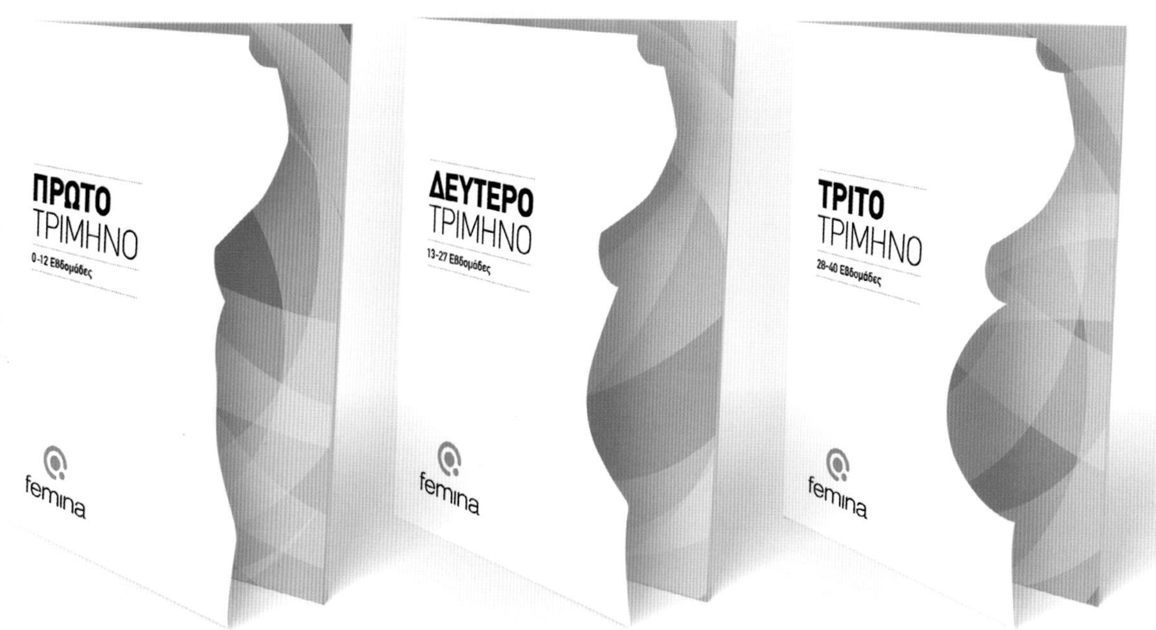

018/
Kanella • *Three brochures for the three phases of pregnancy; the front cover of each brochure series has a unique die-cut that is inspired by the changing shape of a woman's body in each phase of pregnancy*

019/
Fernandez Alvarez® • *Catalogue of light covers for aluminum structure*

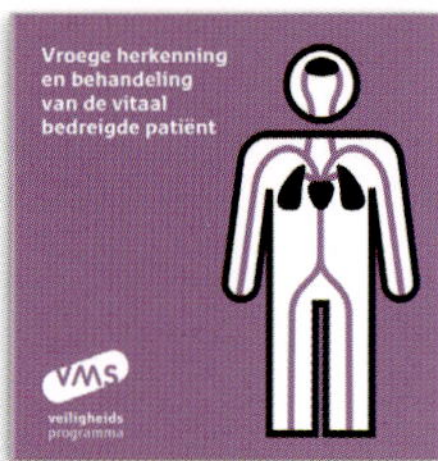

020/
SOGOOD • *Brochure series that put patient safety first. Explaining how the medical staff in hospitals, dealing with different illnesses, can prevent making mistakes, in a simple, clear and sympathetic way*

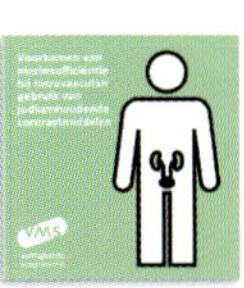
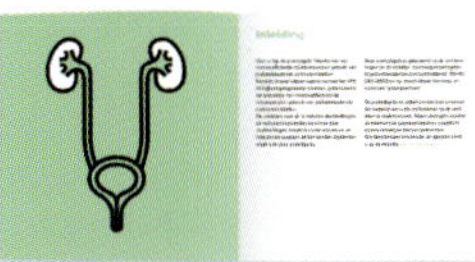

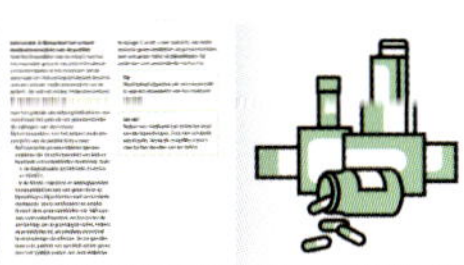
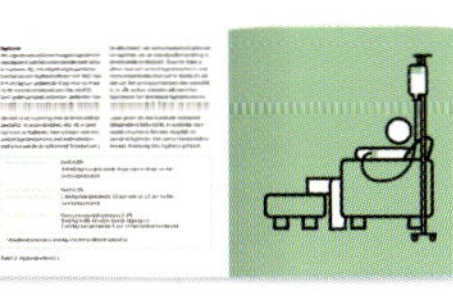

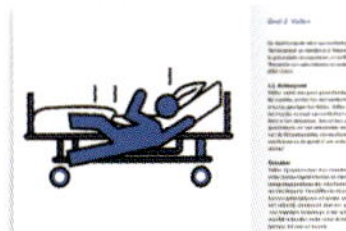

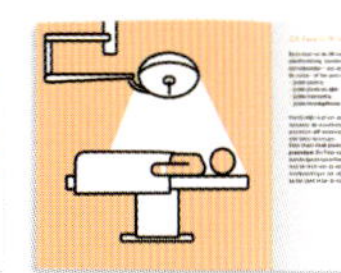

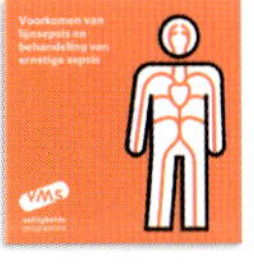

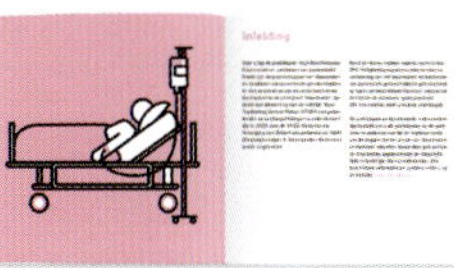

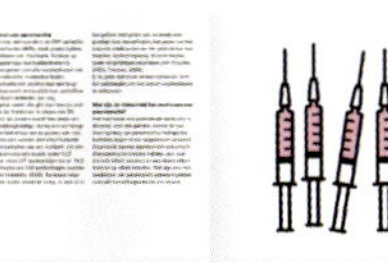
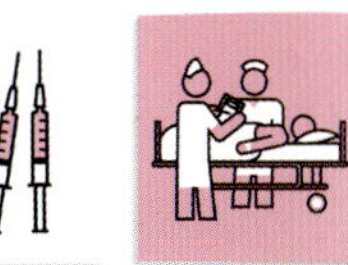

ESPAÑA 2005:
OPCIONES
Y DISYUNTIVAS

10 EL PROBLEMA DEL AGUA:
NO BASTA ENCOMENDARSE
AL SANTO

02 LA SOCIEDAD ESPAÑOLA:
MÁS TOLERANTE

021/
Sonsoles Llorens • *Brochure-offprint for the newspaper La Vanguardia*

022/
rumorvisual • *Brochure series promoting tourism in the province of Cáceres*

023/
David Torrents • *Flyers for Gràfiques Ocultes, a graphic design exhibition*

024/
David Torrents • *Flyers for an exhibition of contemporary circus*

025/
Murray agencia de diseño • *Monthly cultural agenda*

026/
Oxigen comunicació gràfica • *Agendas printed in one colour and black*

027/
Sonsoles Llorens • *Collection of pamphlets highlighting the artistry of Escofet products*

escofet
PAVIMENTOS
escofet
ELEMENTOS DE PROYECTO I
escofet
EMENTOS DE PROYECTO II
escofet
COR-TEN

Dúctil • *2007-2008 catalogue of Christmas and New Year festivals*

UN NADAL
SENSE FRONTERES,
UN PROGRAMA
ENTRE CULTURES

BENVOLGUTS
VEÏNES
I
VEÏNS

LES TRADICIONS
DE NADAL A
ALTRES PAÏSOS
DEL MÓN

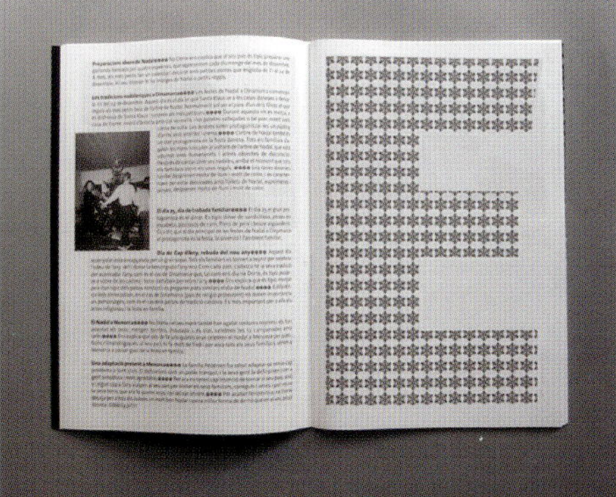

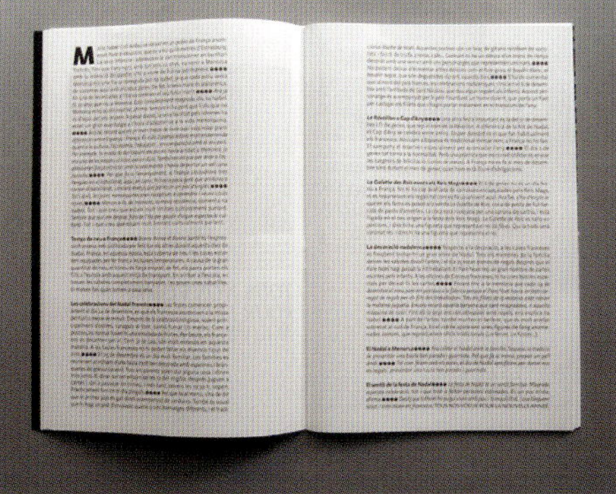

029/
BATLLEGROUP • *An array of design study catalogues*

bau 2010/11
bau nit
Diploma en Disseny Bau Nit
Disseny Gràfic
Disseny d'Interiors

disseny gràfic
i comunicació visual
diseño gráfico
y comunicación visual
disseny gràfic
i comunicació visual

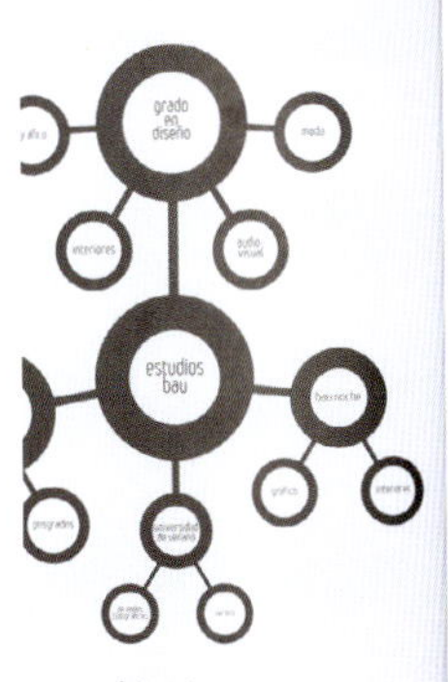
grado en diseño
estudios bau
académica
masters y posgrados
masters & postgraduate degrees
grado en diseño
european bachelor's degree in design
diploma en diseño bau noche
diploma in design "bau evening"
universidad de verano y C.L.E.
summer university and free choice credits (FCC)

030/
Bisgràfic • *Catalogue of children's furniture that is singular for its aesthetic lines and color notes*

entra en un mundo de
colores, de princesas rosas y
príncipes azules en caballos
rojos, de cielos verdes y
nubes amarillas.
entra y descubre sueños
naranjas entre planetas
púrpuras.

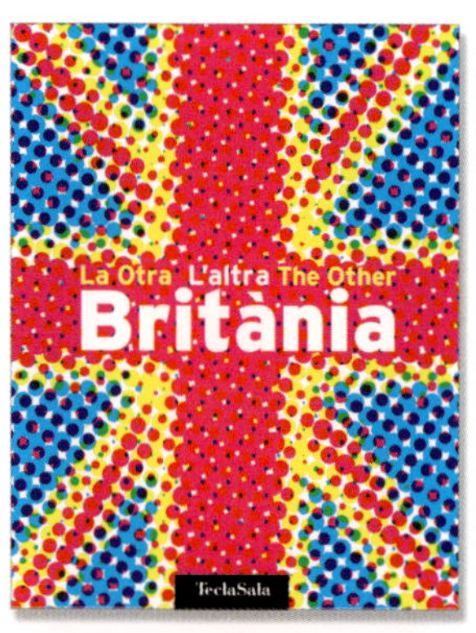

031/

Sonsoles Llorens • *A pop-art rendering of "Union Jack" conveys an atmosphere of vanguard for this exhibition on the new generation of contemporary British artists*

032/
Villuendas+Gómez Disseny • *Promotional and informative pamphlet that outlines programming of the radio station*

033/
elDiseñador s.c.p. • *Flyers for Le Merídien Barcelona, Le POPBARw*

Le POPBAR
DJ SHAKIRA
VESÍCULA DJ'S
DJ IVO
DJ BORJA
DJ BORJA
LUI Solo 12's
DJ GONZO
LLUIS S. CEPRIAN
N&AF
DJ BORJA
DJ BORJA
BAUGHMAN vs LUI
Da Hit Soirée!!
¡NEW YEARS
EVE PARTY!!

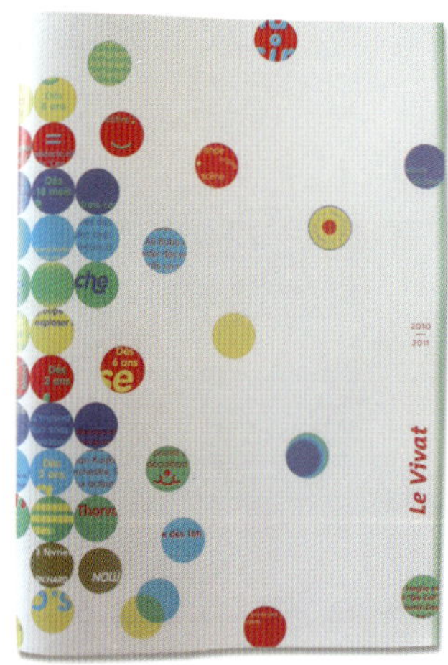

034/
BENBENWORLD • *2010-2011 season catalogue for the theatre Le Vivat*

La femme sans passé

Ch'ti Lyrics

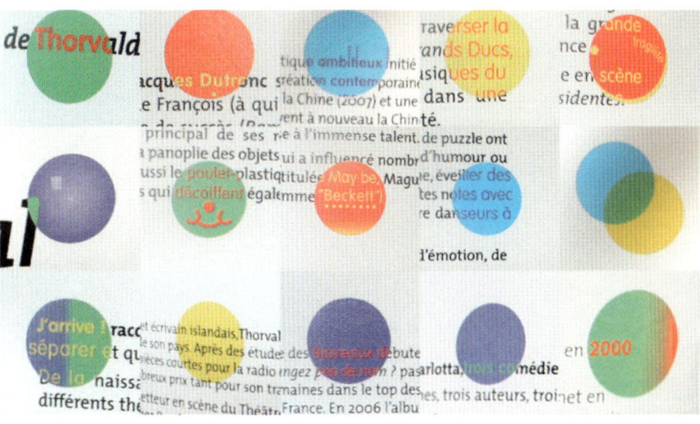
de Thorvald
traverser la
la grande
d'émotion, de
en 2000

Le Vivat

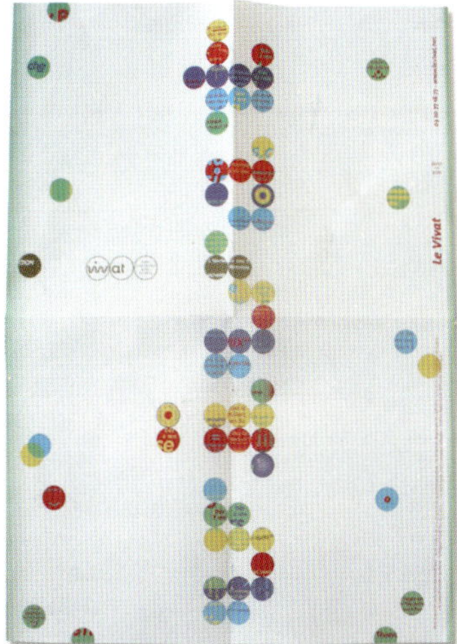
Le Vivat

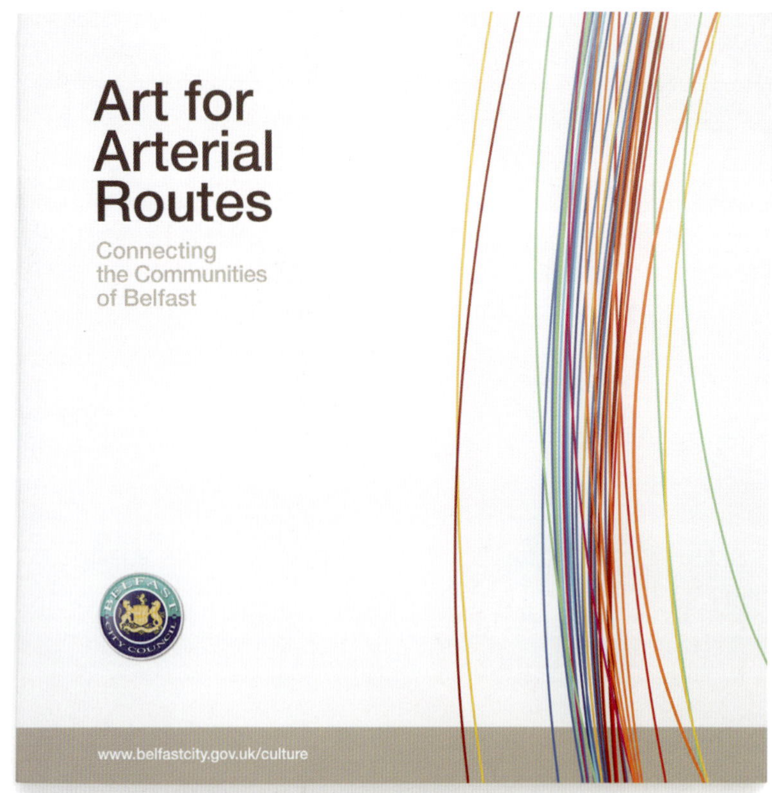

035/
Whitenoise Design Limited • *Brochure documenting art that connects the communities of Belfast*

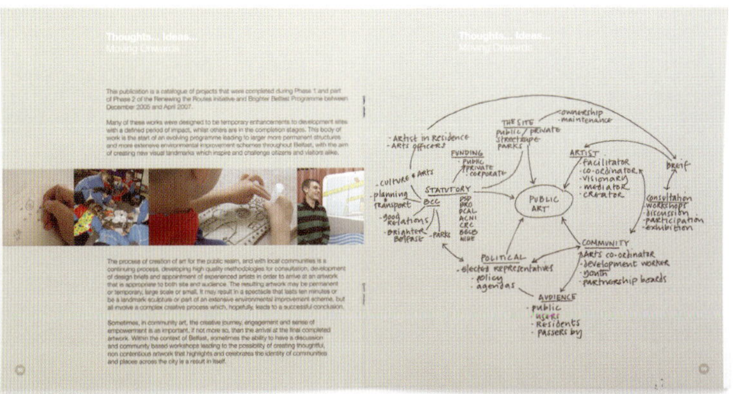

Thoughts... Ideas...

This publication is a catalogue of projects that were completed during Phase 1 and part of Phase 2 of the Renewing the Routes initiative and Brighter Belfast Programme between December 2005 and April 2007.

Many of these works were designed to be temporary enhancements to development sites with a defined period of impact, whilst others are in the completion stages. This body of work is the start of an evolving programme leading to larger more permanent structures and more extensive environmental improvement schemes throughout Belfast, with the aim of creating new visual landmarks which inspire and challenge citizens and visitors alike.

The process of creation of art for the public realm, and with local communities is a continuing process, developing high quality methodologies for consultation, development of design briefs and appointment of experienced artists in order to arrive at an artwork that is appropriate to both site and audience. The resulting artwork may be permanent or temporary, large scale or small. It may result in a spectacle that lasts ten minutes or be a landmark sculpture or part of an extensive environmental improvement scheme, but all involve a complex creative process which, hopefully, leads to a successful conclusion.

Sometimes, in community art, the creative journey, engagement and sense of empowerment is as important, if not more so, than the arrival at the final completed artwork. Within the context of Belfast, sometimes the ability to have a discussion and community based workshops leading to the possibility of creating thoughtful, non contentious artwork that highlights and celebrates the identity of communities and places across the city is a result in itself.

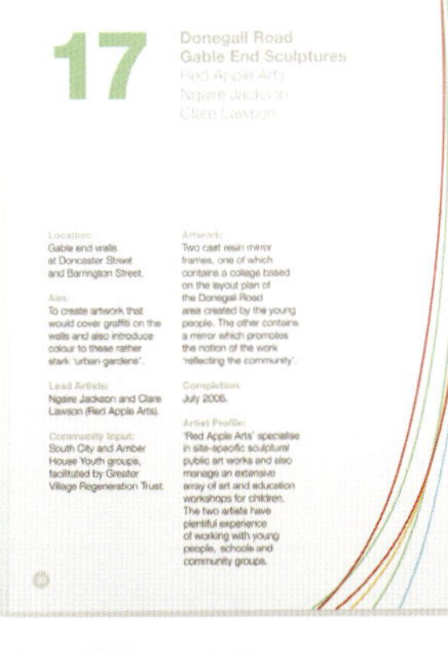

17 Donegall Road Gable End Sculptures
Red Apple Arts
Ngaire Jackson
Clare Lawson

Location:
Gable end walls at Doncaster Street and Barrington Street.

Aim:
To create artwork that would cover graffiti on the walls and also introduce colour to these rather stark 'urban gardens'.

Lead Artists:
Ngaire Jackson and Clare Lawson (Red Apple Arts).

Community Input:
South City and Amber House Youth groups, facilitated by Greater Village Regeneration Trust.

Artwork:
Two cast resin mirror frames, one of which contains a collage based on the layout plan of the Donegall Road area created by the young people. The other contains a mirror which promotes the notion of the work 'reflecting the community'.

Completion:
July 2006.

Artist Profile:
'Red Apple Arts' specialise in site-specific sculptural public art works and also manage an extensive array of art and education workshops for children. The two artists have plentiful experience of working with young people, schools and community groups.

036/
Dandelion • *Brochure explaining the rebrand of Martindale Pharma®*

Be
part
of it.
Brand Book
Martindale Pharma®
part
of it.
Brand Book
Martindale Pharma®

037/
Hoet&Hoet • *Catalogue for Marie's Corner*

and watch

and sip

and work

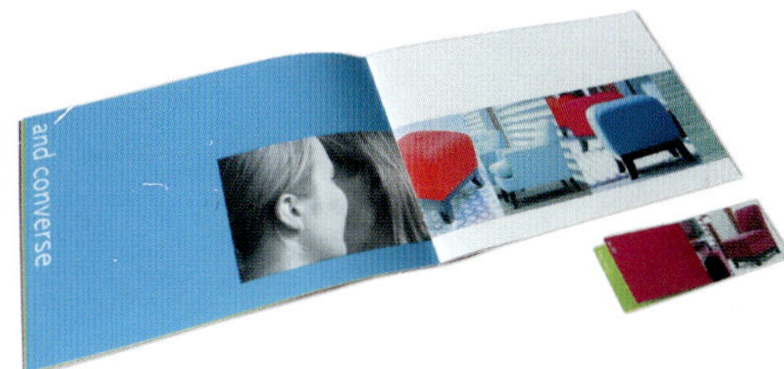
and converse

038/
BENBENWORLD • *Leaflet, detailing the 20-year anniversary of the theatre Le Vivat*

saison 2009-2010 - 03 20 77 18 77 - www.levivat.net

saison 2009-2010 - 03 20 77 18 77 - www.levivat.net

Loin d'être
fini

039/
Murray agencia de diseño • *Brochure promoting Mustang's campaign autumn winter 2008*

mustang
mustang

mustang

mustang

Barfutura • *Pressbook for the film La Isla Interior by Félix Sabroso and Dunia Ayaso*

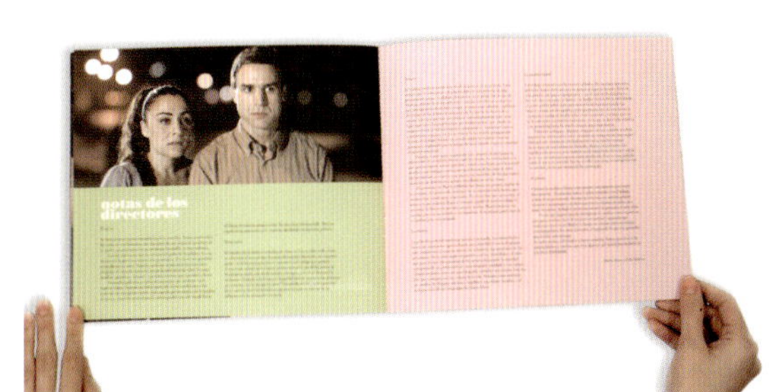
notas de los directores

los actores
CANDELA PEÑA
CELSO BUGALLO
ANTONIO DE LA TORRE

ALBERTO SAN JUAN
CRISTINA MARCOS
GERALDINE CHAPLIN
CELSO BUGALLO
ANTONIO DE LA TORRE

041/
Nifava + Canseixanta • *Design and layout explaining the photo-romance Ramoneta, which was incorporated into the programme of the Banyoles Municipal Theatre of Performing Arts*

Ramoneta
núm.1
setembre/
desembre
2008
Programació d'Arts Escèniques
i Musicals de Banyoles

"UN CIOOOP LA PAASSIÓÓÓ ♫..."
JA M'AGRADA
COM HO FAS,
PERÒ LA
PREFEREIXO A
ELLA.

UN DIA DESPRÉS.
CLINICA SALUS INFIRMORUM DE BANYOLES
HABITACIÓ 118:
QUÈ VOL! TANTS ANYS
A BARCELONA,
AIXÍ HAVIA D'ACABAR!
HABITACIÓ 308:
VA MORIR A L'ACTE,
POBRE PORC.
HABITACIÓ 215:
ÉS LA PETITA DE CAN RAMON.
HABITACIÓ 210:
DIUEN QUE VENIA
A INAUGURAR
NO SÉ QUÈ.
HABITACIÓ 116:
EN TÉ PER MESOS,
S'HA TRENCAT
LA TÍBIA, EL PERONÉ,
EL FÈMUR...

TENS VISITA RAMONETA,
ET VENEN A VEURE DE
L'AJUNTAMENT...
RECUPERA'T. TRANQUIL·LA,
JA TENIM SUBSTITUT PER
L'ESPECTACLE D'INAUGURACIÓ.
AMB QUÈ INAUGURAREM
L'AUDITORI ARA?!
JA ENS
INVENTAREM
ALGUNA COSA...
CONTINUARÀ.

"... ♩ POT MÉÉÉS QUE LA FOOOR..."
SI M'HAN ESCOLLIT COM
A PROTAGONISTA ÉS PERQUÈ
SÓC MILLOR QUE ELLA!
CALMA'T, RAMONETA,
QUE AIXÒ ÉS NOMÉS
UN ESPECTACLE DE POBLE!
EL HE ESTAT ESTUDIANT
5 ANYS A BARCELONA...
SI HAS ESTAT ESTUDIANT
ÉS GRÀCIES AL MEU PIS!
CALLA I MIRA LA
CARRETERA,
QUE T'HAS
SALTAT
EL TRENCANT!

AQUESTA PORQUERIA
DE MÚSICA
M'HA DESPISTAT!
TU SI QUE ETS...
UN PORC!!!
MERDA!
OINC, OINC!*

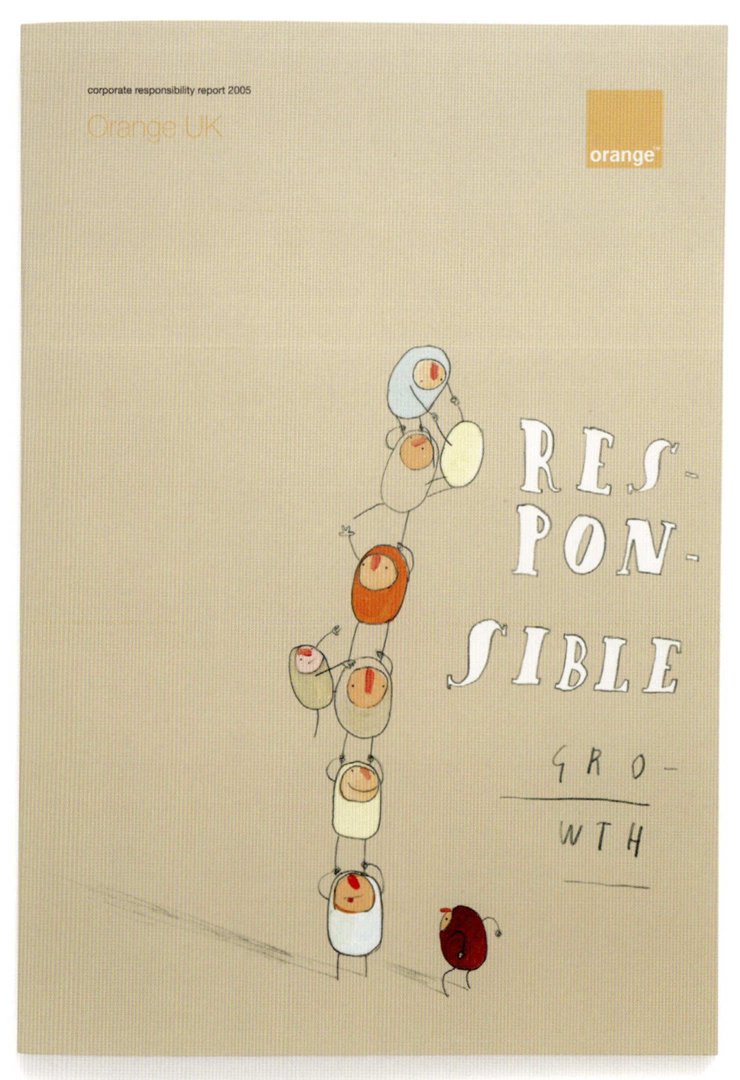

042/
Whitenoise Design Limited • *Illustrated brochure for the 2005 corporate responsibility report for Orange UK*

managing waste
responding to global events in 2006
GLOBAL EVENTS

our network performance
managing access to adult content
CAN YOU HEAR ME?
CONTENT

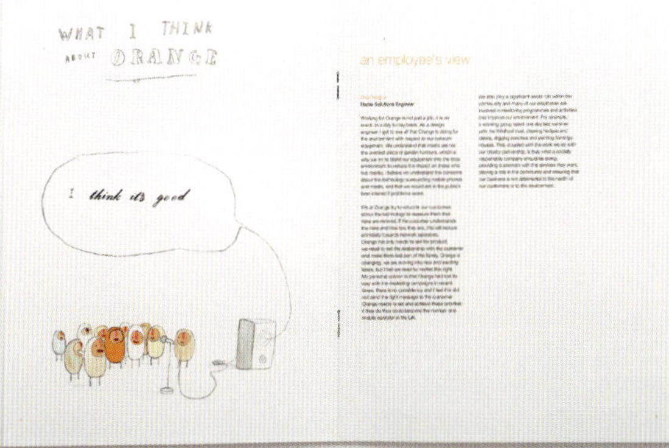
WHAT I THINK ABOUT ORANGE
an employee's view
I think it's good

043/
La Camorra • *Pamphlet for a 2009 conference organised by la Fundación Española para la Ciencia y la Tecnología (FECYT) and Institute Cervantes*

044/
seesponge • *Catalogue and sales tool of the product line of Yarema Marquetry, a designer and manufacturer of semi-custom wood inlays*

extra! • *Corporate brochure and annual report*

El Col·legi
dels professionals
del Medi Ambient

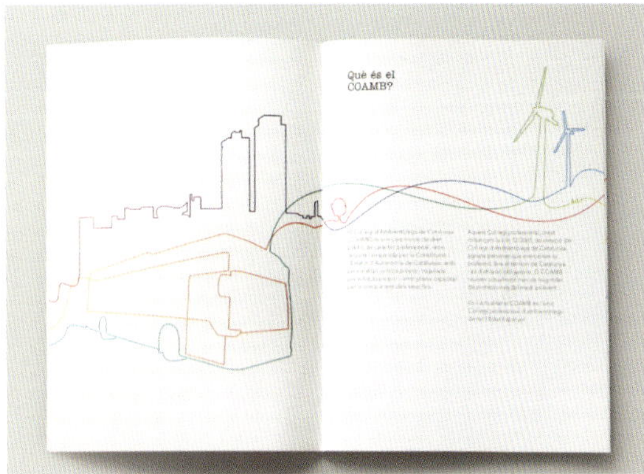
Què és el
COAMB?

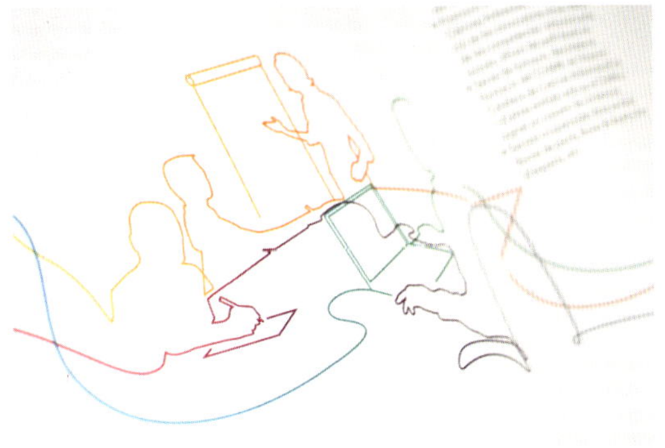

El Col·legi
dels professionals
del Medi Ambient

046/
Whitenoise Design Limited • *Brochure design for the H.E.A.P. Chart - a hierarchy of earnings, attributes and privilege analysis*

THE H.E.A.P. CHART
Hierarchy of Earnings, Attributes and Privilege Analysis

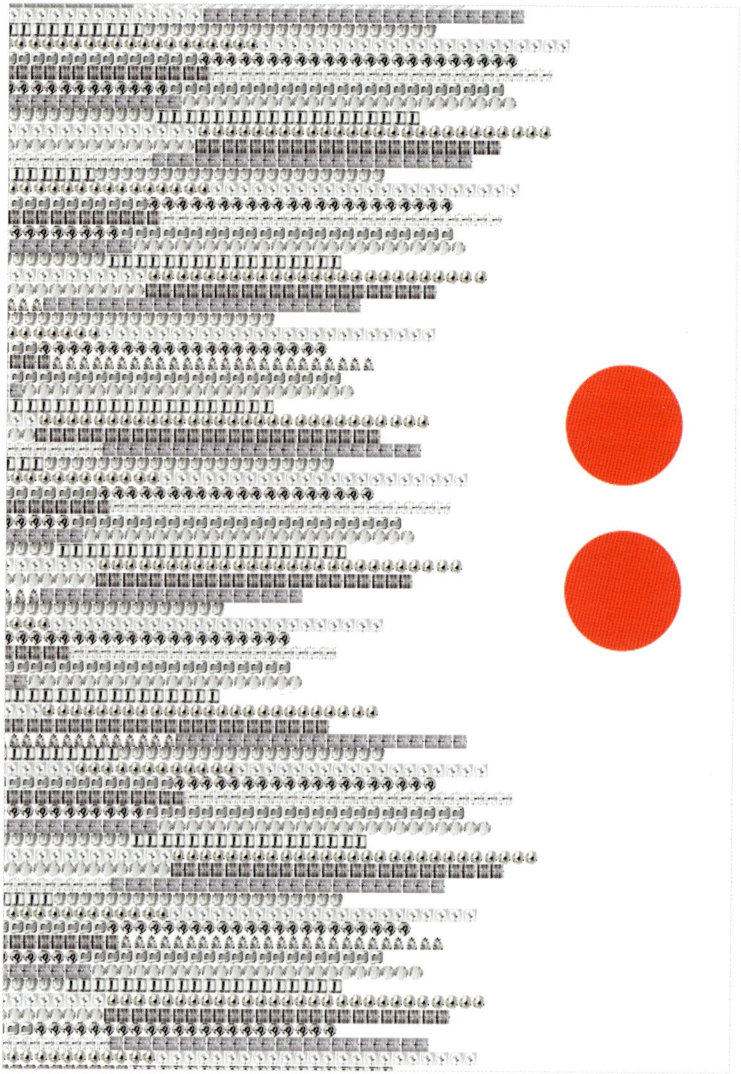

047/
FK Design srl • *General catalogue Fabbian Illuminazione*

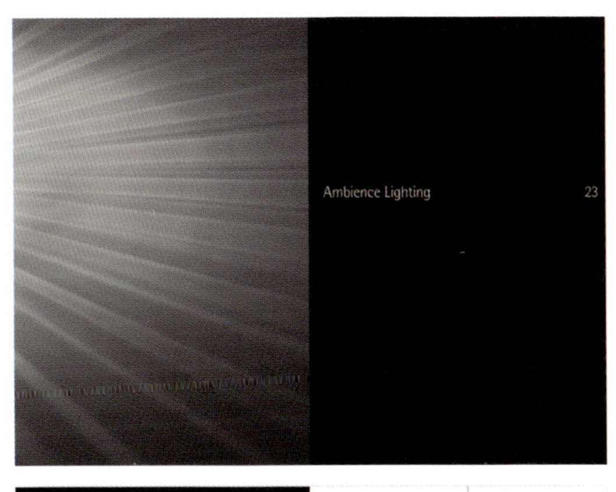
Ambience Lighting
23

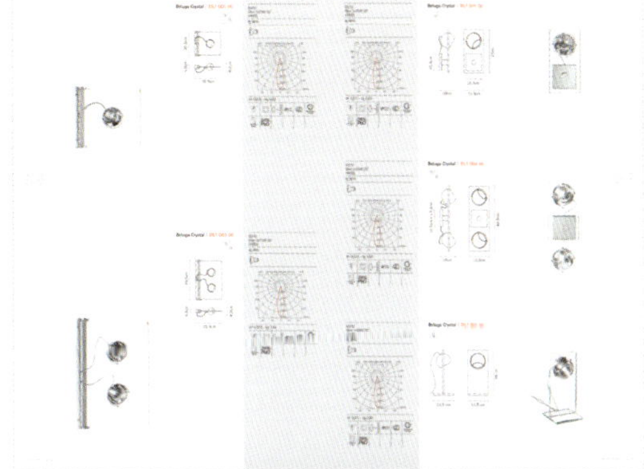

Beluga Steel
D57

90 technicians, workers, researchers and young designers

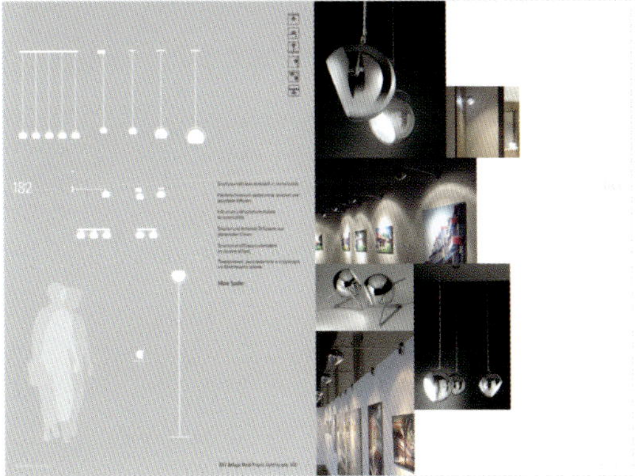
182

36

toormix

TOORMIX LATEST PROJECTS POSTER

2007-2009

A, B.

- AECID (Agencia Española de Cooperación Internacional para el Desarrollo)
- ADG-FAD
- Ajuntament de Barcelona
- Ajuntament de Pals
- Áreas
- Arturo Álvarez
- Auna
- BOMA

C.

- Camper
- CCCB
- CEPA (Centre d'Ecologia i Projectes Alternatius)
- Ceprocoop
- Contrapunto

D.

- Desigual
- DDI. Sociedad Estatal para el Desarrollo del Diseño y la Innovación

F.

- FAD (Foment de les Arts i el Disseny)
- Fundació Bosch i Gimpera
- Fundación Small
- Fundació Social del Raval

G.

- Galeria Alea
- Galvarplast Automotive
- Generalitat de Catalunya – Entitat Autònoma de Difusió Cultural
- Grafiko
- Grupo TTD

I, J.

- ICUB (Institut de Cultura de Barcelona)
- IL3 · Universitat de Barcelona
- Imira Entertainment
- Institut Ramon Llull
- JORGC (Col·legi de Joiers de Catalunya)

L.

- La Pedrera / Laie
- Layetana Inmobiliaria
- Loewe
- Lorena Films

M.

- Mahou · San Miguel
- Matutano – Pepsico
- Menta
- Mercat de les Flors
- MAEC (Ministerio de Asuntos Exteriores y de Cooperación)
- MTV España
- MHCB (Museu d'Història de la Ciutat de Barcelona)

N, P.

- Nike
- Planet Hair

S, T.

- Sagrera TV
- Samsung
- Scartissue Magazine
- Teatro Circo Price
- Telefónica

R.

- Random House Mondadori
- Reckitt-Benckiser
- Retevisión

V.

- Virreina Centre de la Imatge

048/
Toormix • *Publication-type portfolio with a selection of the most recent projects of the studio*

TOORMIX
LATEST
PROJECTS
POSTER
2007-2009

ALGUNS PROJECTES:
CLIENTS DE TOOR-MIX:

PA-PERS
02
PAPERS ON PLASMAR PROJECTES DE CREATIVITAT REALISTA®. PAPERS ÚTILS

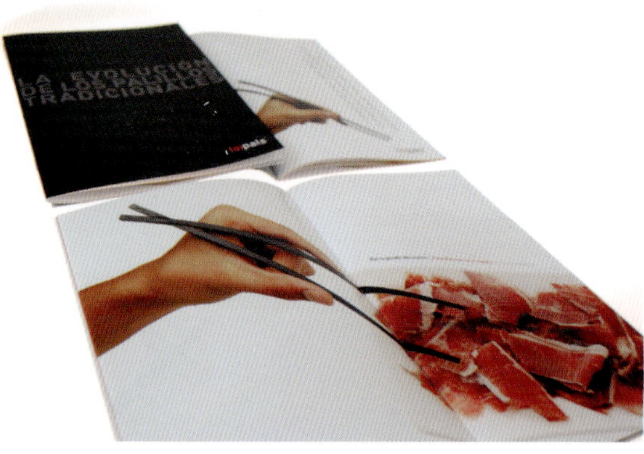

049/
neura projectes • *Promotional catalog*

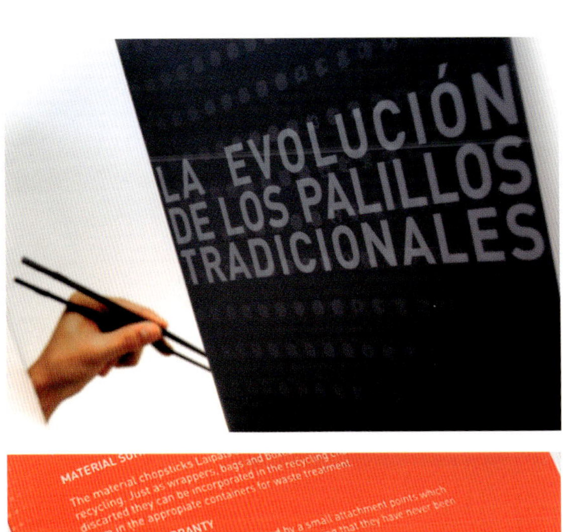
LA EVOLUCIÓN
DE LOS PALILLOS
TRADICIONALES

L'EVOLUCIÓ DELS PALS TRADICIONALS
LA EVOLUCIÓN DE LOS PALILLOS TRADICIONALES
THE EVOLUTION OF TRADITIONAL CHOPSTICKS
DE LOS PALILLOS
TRADICIONALES

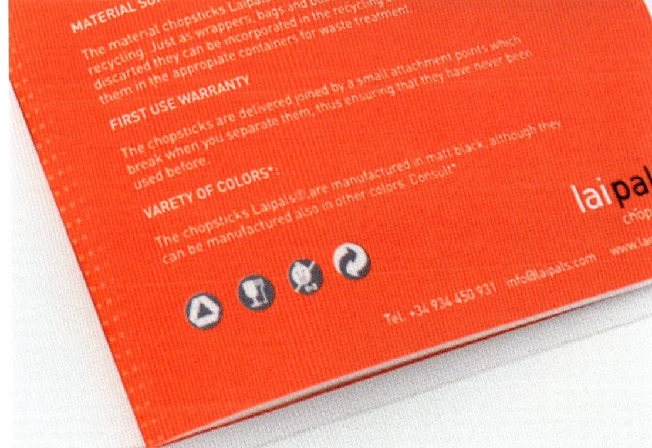
them in the appropriate containers for waste treatment.
FIRST USE WARRANTY
The chopsticks are delivered joined by a small attachment points which
break when you separate them, thus ensuring that they have never been
used before.
VARETY OF COLORS*:
The chopsticks Laipals® are manufactured in matt black, although they
can be manufactured also in other colors. Consult*
Tel. +34 934 450 931 info@laipals.com

LA EVOLUCIÓN
DE LOS PALILLOS
TRADICIONALES
laipals

050/
BURO-GDS • *Booklet documenting the student exchange program participation by three schools in France and Thailand*

BETWEEN
PARIS+
BANGKOK

SOMMAIRE
CONTENTS

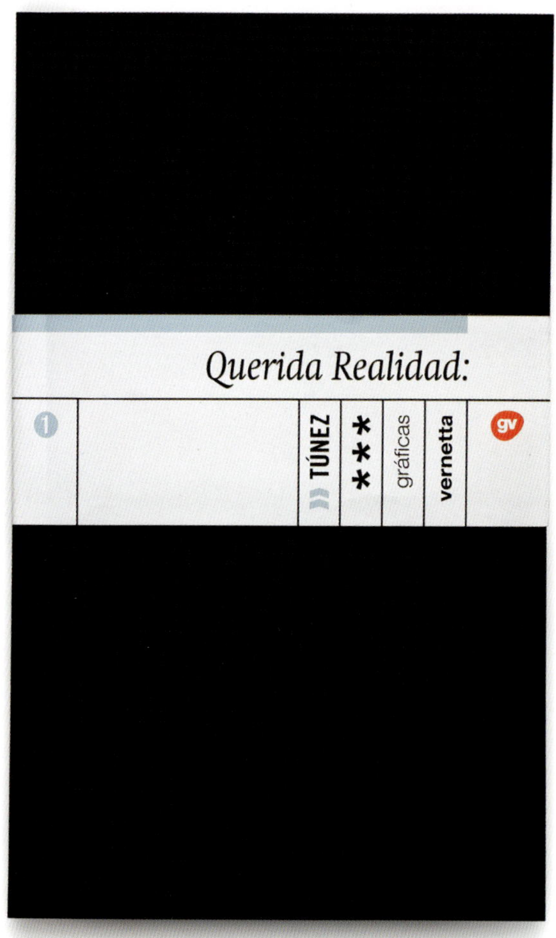

051/
Juan Martinez Estudio • *Promotional publication*

También podré pasar por la aduana un par de bolsas grandes llenas de experiencias y sensaciones muy diversas: la tarde de lluvia tomando el té de menta en la medina, la conversación con los zapateros de la casba, los cigarrillos en el puerto de Hammamet, nadar de noche en la isla de Yerba, comer, dormir...

¿Cómo voy a tener la seguridad de que la luz y los colores serán los mismos que estoy ahora viendo? Y los matices, los reflejos, los grises, los infinitos matices de blancos, de ocres...

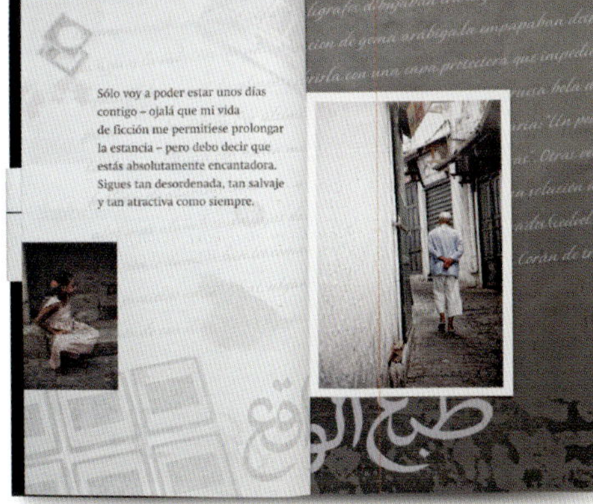
Sólo voy a poder estar unos días contigo – ojalá que mi vida de ficción me permitiese prolongar la estancia – pero debo decir que estás absolutamente encantadora. Sigues tan desordenada, tan salvaje y tan atractiva como siempre.

052/
Xavier Martínez Balet • *2008-09 programme for Fundación Taller de Guionistas*

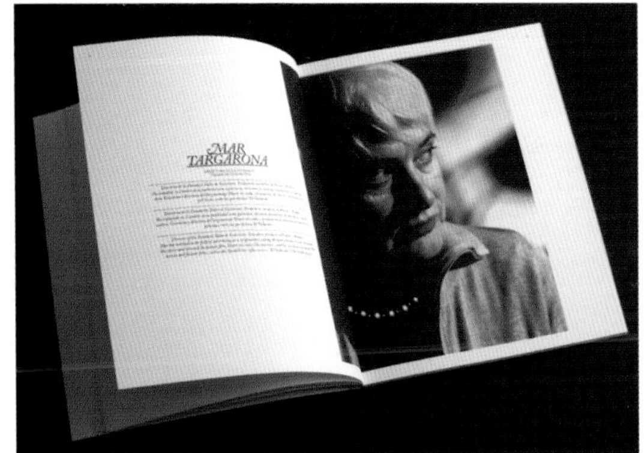
MAR
TARGARONA

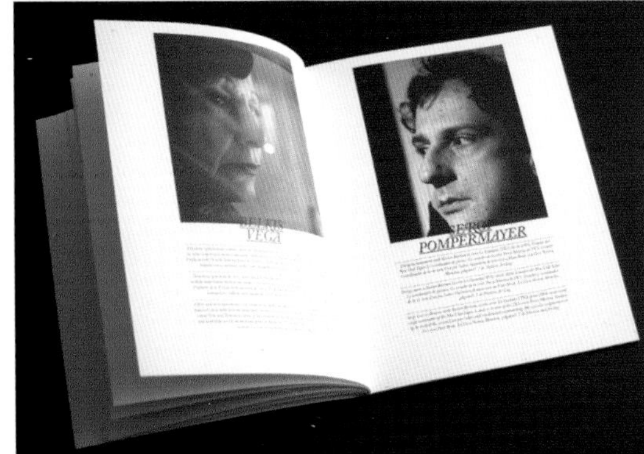
VEGA
POMPERMAYER

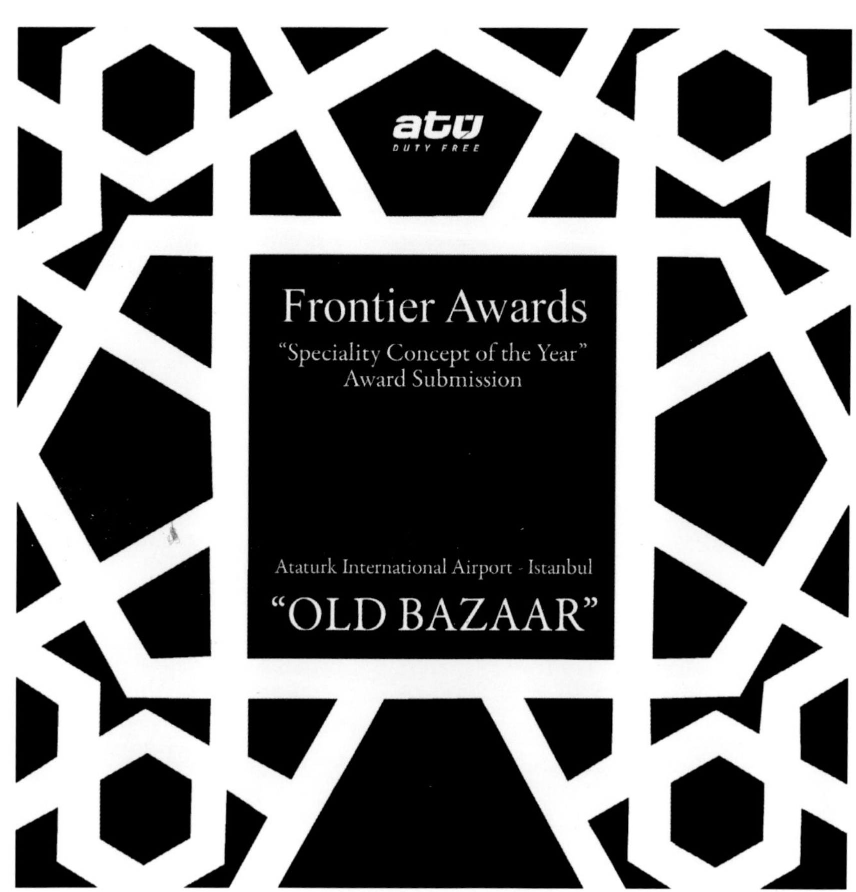

053/
2FRESH • *Brochure for ATU honouring Frontier Awards*

Thank you for your
kind attention...

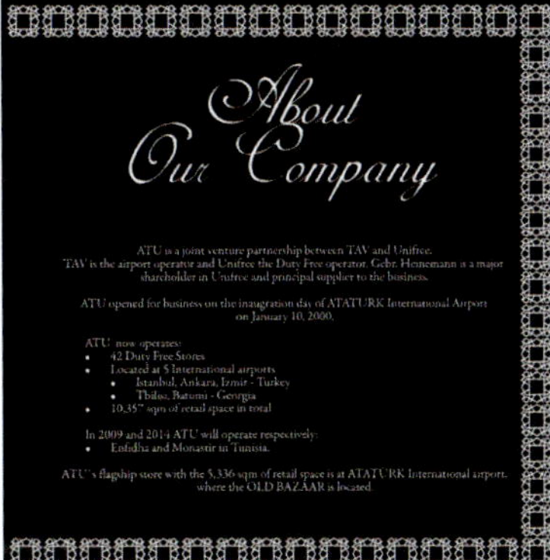
About
Our Company
ATU is a joint venture partnership between TAV and Unifree.
TAV is the airport operator and Unifree the Duty Free operator. Gebr. Heinemann is a major shareholder in Unifree and principal supplier to the business.
ATU opened for business on the inaugration day of ATATURK International Airport on January 10, 2000.
ATU now operates:
42 Duty Free Stores
Located at 5 International airports
Istanbul, Ankara, Izmir - Turkey
Tbilisi, Batumi - Georgia
10,357 sqm of retail space in total
In 2009 and 2014 ATU will operate respectively:
Enfidha and Monastir in Tunisia.
ATU's flagship store with the 5,336 sqm of retail space is at ATATURK International airport, where the OLD BAZAAR is located.

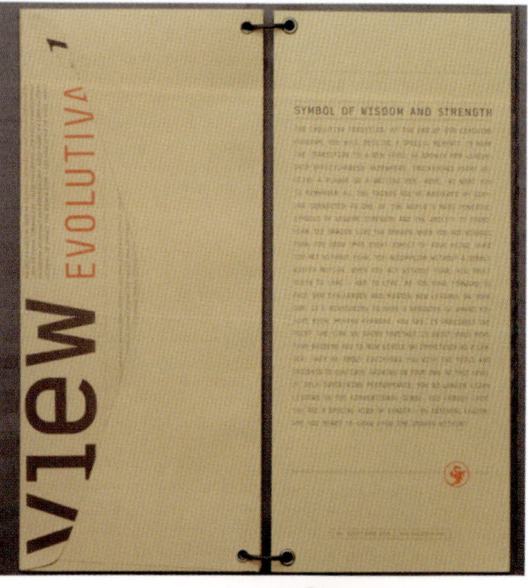

054/
Blok Design • *Brochure designed in a book format for a company that specialises in leadership coaching*

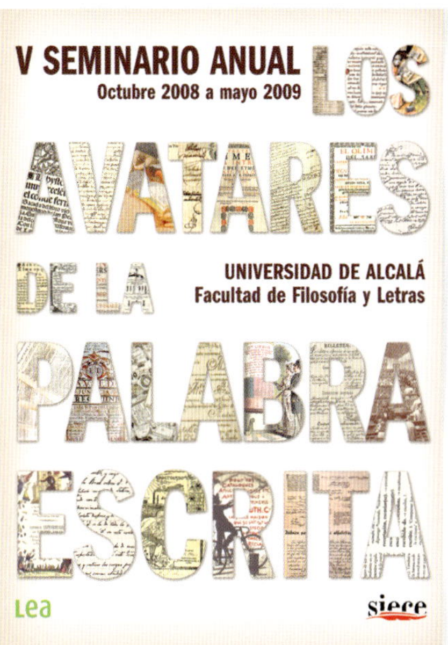

055/
Carol García del Busto • *Design for the 5th annual seminar on the history of the written word, hosted by Universidad de Alcalá*

056/
Barfutura • *Pressbook with 72 pages for the film El Mal Ajeno*

SINOPSIS
SYNOPSIS

REPARTO
CAST

EDUARDO
NORIEGA
Diego

Single Fold

057/
FK Design srl • *Brochure promoting the line of shaving brushes from Acca Kappa*

IL CIUFFO
THE TIP

Flessibile, morbidissimo e resistente, realizzato con il miglior pelo di tasso argentato, il ciuffo è garanzia di lunga vita al pennello. Con la sua dolcezza e naturalezza, oltre alle caratteristiche dermoaffini, assicura una saponatura ricca, compatta, omogenea e un piacevole e benefico massaggio che prepara la pelle a una rasatura perfetta. Il suo colore neutro e caldo si intensifica [illegible] profonde che sfumano nell'avorio, per culminare con un'elegantissima chioma dai riflessi argentei.

Flexible, soft and hardwearing, and made of superior silver badger bristle, the tip guarantees the long life of the brush.
Soft, natural and skin friendly, the tip will generate a thick, smooth lather and massage the skin gently but beneficially to prepare it for a perfect shave.
Its warm, neutral tones are intensified in softly seductive, deep shades that fade away into the [illegible] silver-tipped brush head.

LE FORME
THE FORM

Scolpito a mano in forme di squisita arte italiana, il design applicato alla semplicità degli oggetti del nostro quotidiano produce effetti magici.
Ora rigorosamente geometriche, ora leggere e sinuose, in Collezione Privata lo studio delle forme è frutto di una ricerca stilistica che si esprime attraverso l'armonia e la proporzione e non dimentica la funzionalità dell'oggetto. La forma è determinante per il successo della rasatura, a cominciare dall'impugnatura ergonomica che facilita le manovre del rito, assecondando la mano e seguendo le forme del viso, con un risultato impeccabile.

Hand sculpted into the fine forms of exquisite Italian art, design principles are applied to simple everyday objects to produce breathtaking effects.
At times meticulously geometrical, at times light and sinewy, the study of form in Collezione Privata is the result of a pursuit of style conveyed through harmony and proportion, without overlooking the function of the object.
Form is the key to a successful shave, starting from the ergonomic grip which facilitates the ritual's gestures, assisting the hand and following the contours of the face, to produce impeccable results.

L'ARTE DEL FARSI LA BARBA
THE ART OF SHAVING

La rasatura di una volta è oggi consacrata a rito, in un cerimoniale che si celebra nell'arte del farsi la barba. Irrinunciabile momento di piacere, pausa di riflessione edonistica per riscoprire e assaporare il ritmo lento della vita di un tempo, sigla il recupero di una gestualità perduta, dove spazio e tempo si fondono in momenti intimi e privatissimi e l'igiene personale s'intreccia con la scultura, in una surreale atmosfera sul cui sfondo si muove il protagonista assoluto, il pennello di Collezione Privata.

The old-fashioned shave has now become a ritual celebrated in the modern art of shaving.
This sacrosanct moment of pleasure is a pause for hedonistic meditation where the easy pace of times gone by can be savoured. It represents the revival of long-lost habits, where time and space come together in moments of pure, intimate pleasure, and where personal grooming becomes like painting on an imaginary canvas, with the brush strokes made by a Collezione Privata brush.

IL PENNELLO ACCA KAPPA
ACCA KAPPA BRUSH

Depositario di un'arte italiana che da 130 anni si tramanda segretamente di generazione in generazione, il pennello Acca Kappa "Collezione Privata" è realizzato secondo i codici di un'elevata ricerca estetica. Ogni pezzo, con la sua forte identità espressiva, racconta la storia di persone, materiali nobili e cultura artigiana italiana ed esprime il talento artistico e la passione profusa dal suo maestro.

Embodiment of an Italian art that has been secretly passed on from generation to generation for over 130 years, the Acca Kappa "Collezione Privata" brush is made to the very highest of aesthetic standards. The strongly individual presence of each piece tells the story of people, noble materials and the history of Italian craftsmanship, an expression of the artistic talent and passion that went into its making.

058/
oikos associati • *Promotional brochure for CLEAF, an Italy-based designer, manufacturer, and finisher of surfaces for interior design*

alta tecnologia e qualità
high technology and quality

CLEAF

Dalla tecnica alle emozioni
CLEAF

059/
Logoorange Design Studio • *40pages brochure for Education International, a global federation of teacher unions*

teachers and trade unionists were well-represented among the 35,000.

EDUCATION INTERNATIONAL

Teachers and trade unionists were well-represented among the 35,000 demonstrators who marched through the streets of London on 28 March to demand that leaders.

Teachers and trade unionists were well-represented among the 35,000 demonstrators who marched through the streets of London on 28 March to demand that leaders of the G20 make the needs of working people and the poor top priority when they meet this week to draft a global.

Teachers and trade unionists were well-represented among the 35,000 demonstrators who marched through the streets of London on 28 March to demand that leaders of the G20 make the needs of working people and the poor top priority when they meet this week to draft a global

Teachers and trade unionists were well-represented among the 35,000 demonstrators who marched through the streets of London on 28 March to demand that leaders of the G20 make the needs of working people and the poor top priority when they meet this week to draft a global.

getting the world to work: Global Union strategies for recovery

03

getting the world to work: Global Union strategies for recovery

Page 47 Teachers join in call for G20 to put people first
Page 51 Keeping Schools Safe
Page 54 Invest in education to mitigate economic crisis, EI leaders say
Page 47 Teachers join in call for G20 to put people first

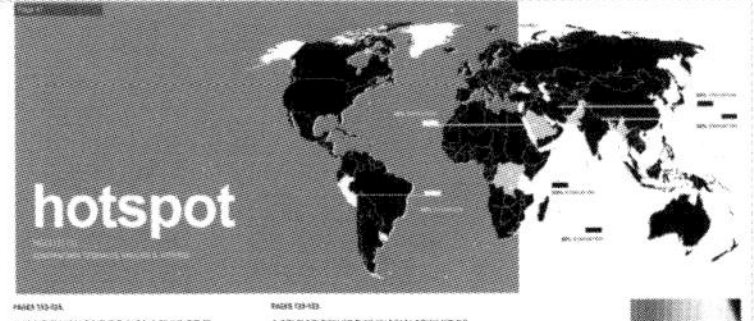

A COMPARISON OF THE PHARMACOKINETICS OF TWO DIFFERENT FORMULATIONS OF EXTENDED-RELEASE NIACIN

OPTIMISING IMMUNE TOLERANCE INDUCTION STRATEGIES IN THE MANAGEMENT OF HAEMOPHILIA PATIENTS WITH INHIBITORS: A COST-MINIMISATION ANALYSIS

CARBAPENEMS VERSUS OTHER BETA-LACTAMS IN THE TREATMENT OF HOSPITALISED PATIENTS WITH INFECTION: A MIXED TREATMENT COMPARISON

CARBAPENEMS VERSUS OTHER BETA-LACTAMS IN THE TREATMENT OF HOSPITALISED PATIENTS WITH INFECTION: A MIXED TREATMENT COMPARISON

A COMPARISON OF THE PHARMACOKINETICS OF TWO DIFFERENT FORMULATIONS OF EXTENDED-RELEASE NIACIN

OPTIMISING IMMUNE TOLERANCE INDUCTION STRATEGIES IN THE MANAGEMENT OF HAEMOPHILIA PATIENTS WITH INHIBITORS: A COST-MINIMISATION ANALYSIS

CARBAPENEMS VERSUS OTHER BETA-LACTAMS IN THE TREATMENT OF HOSPITALISED PATIENTS WITH INFECTION: A MIXED TREATMENT COMPARISON

CARBAPENEMS VERSUS OTHER BETA-LACTAMS IN THE TREATMENT OF HOSPITALISED PATIENTS WITH INFECTION: A MIXED TREATMENT COMPARISON

CARBAPENEMS VERSUS OTHER BETA-LACTAMS IN THE TREATMENT OF HOSPITALISED PATIENTS WITH INFECTION: A MIXED TREATMENT COMPARISON

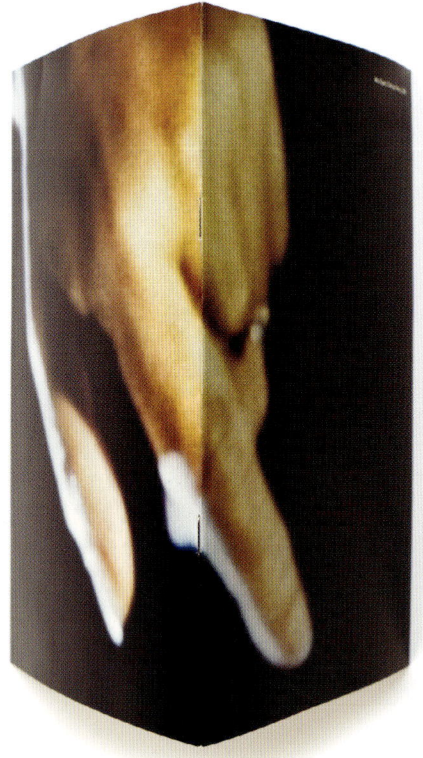

060/
El vivero • *Pamphlet describing the Alia Syed exhibition at El Museo Nacional Centro de Arte Reina Sofía*

Alia Syed

Imagine your own history

Back in 2004, while in New York, I went to see the exhibition of Alia Syed in a small gallery located near Union Square on the East Side – the opposite side to Chelsea, which, in those days, people believed was the only neighborhood where you could see "art." The exhibition at the Talwar Gallery comprised only one work: *Eating Grass*. My curiosity about the London-based Syed was sparked by a short review in the New York Times by Holland Cotter – perhaps the only reviewer on this paper who writes about "minority" artists. To him, *Eating Grass* was visually enticing through its luminosity of "pure white light [that] floods the screen which may or may not be the equivalent of a blinding nuclear blast... a film that filters a richly-colored history through a visionary prism."

Cotter was right. The film's amazing sense of style and form slips through our fingers like fluid, but hidden behind its deeply-saturated colors is a real story. I always remember this gorgeous film zooming in and out and around the action because of its complete freedom of movement – as well as those sibilant voices on the sound track saying something so softly, so disjointedly, that it could hardly be heard or indeed understood. Later I learned that the sound consisted of lines spoken in Urdu and English – story lines written by Syed, who was born in Swansea, Wales (UK) of Indian and Welsh descent.

But there is no need to understand the spoken words in order to follow the rhythmic sequences that cut across the traditional boundaries between filmmakers and their subjects. The stories refer to the five-times-a-day prescribed for Muslim prayer and the words are, like Cotter says, as "impressionistic as the images themselves". Poetic and political, *Eating Grass* carries a specific reference to a promise made in 1974 by President Zulfikar Ali Bhutto of Pakistan, who said that his country would have nuclear weapons like those of India, even if Pakistanis had to eat grass to finance them. In a deliberate endeavor to avoid sinking under the weight of heavily-charged violent images, the film's political connection is not apparent. A piece extracted from the stream of life, accumulating images of people and places, it reveals its political reference only in its title.

Eating Grass, 2003, 16mm, sound, 22'52"
Swan, 1987, 16mm, without sound, 4'

12 de febrero a 13 de abril de 2009
Edificio Sabatini. Calle Santa Isabel, 52

www.museoreinasofia.es

Museo Nacional Centro de Arte **Reina Sofía**

Shot in Karachi and Lahore (Pakistan) and in London, the film seems an endless sequence of private and public spaces, from homes adorned with flower pots to a noisy, busy street market. The dreamlike imagery lacks chronology and its stylistic bricolage intensifies reality, opening a window onto life. *Eating Grass* is an abstraction of a political documentary film, sometimes bringing to mind *A Tale of Love* by another "minority" filmmaker, the Vietnamese Trinh T. Minh-ha. Both films reveal influence from the collagists and other experimental filmmakers of the 1960s – although *A Tale of Love* is built around Minh-ha's concerns: the female body and issues of subjectivity, race and class in a post-colonial world.

Syed's first exhibition in Spain also includes the earlier *Swan*, "a sensual insinuation" as it was once defined. It relates to the avant-garde filmmakers and their interest in depicting nature, or more importantly, using nature as a visual metaphor for the expression of human subjectivity.[1] The luxurious images of a white swan preparing for flight are extremely well-composed, like photographs. The swan's movement, repeatedly extending and folding its wings allows the viewer to contemplate the incongruence of moment. Although the film seems to be representing the swan spreading its wings before flight, it doesn't represent anything, but creates a new narrative out of the void. Since there is nothing without meaning – and regardless of the difference in content and film technique – both *Eating Grass* and *Swan* offer viewers a unique opportunity: to imagine their own history.

Berta Sichel

Curated by: Berta Sichel, Departamento de Audiovisuales

061/
MusaWorkLab • *Catalogue for the Underconstruction exhibition from the artist Mónica de Miranda*

UNDER —
CONSTRUCTION
MÓNICA DE MIRANDA
PAUL GOODWIN

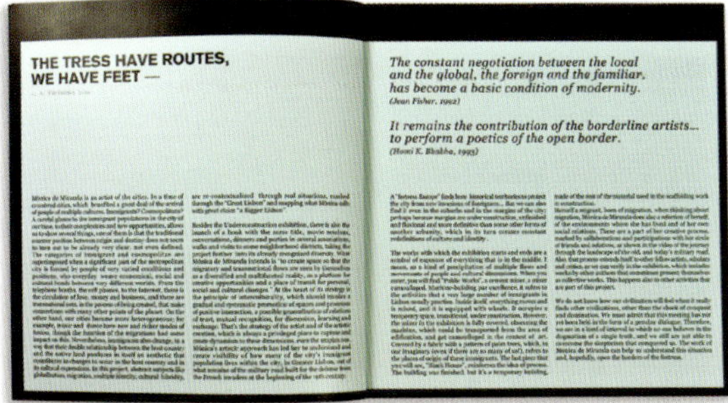
THE TRESS HAVE ROUTES,
WE HAVE FEET —
The constant negotiation between the local and the global, the foreign and the familiar, has become a basic condition of modernity.
(Jean Fisher, 1992)
It remains the contribution of the borderline artists... to perform a poetics of the open border.
(Homi K. Bhabha, 1993)

Paradise

Logoorange Design Studio • *Type R Magazine brochure*

NIKKI LAUDA

STAT ... O ... PLAY

MY GENERAL GRAPHIC DESIGN IS INFLUENCED BY MODERNISM AND THE NEW YORK SCHOOL, YET I STILL HOPE TO DISCOVER SOMETHING IN MYSELF THAT IS TRULY AN INNOVATIVE AND TOTALLY ORIGINAL STYLE

063/
Grupo Anton Comunicación / 6 Sombreros Creativos / Diseño: Fuensanta Blanca • *Book presenting the of works of Torregrosa*

064/
Alambre Estudio • *Promotional catalogue for the new collection of VITA bath*

065/
Dúctil • *Dossier that containing the proposal of activities and schedules for an international congress*

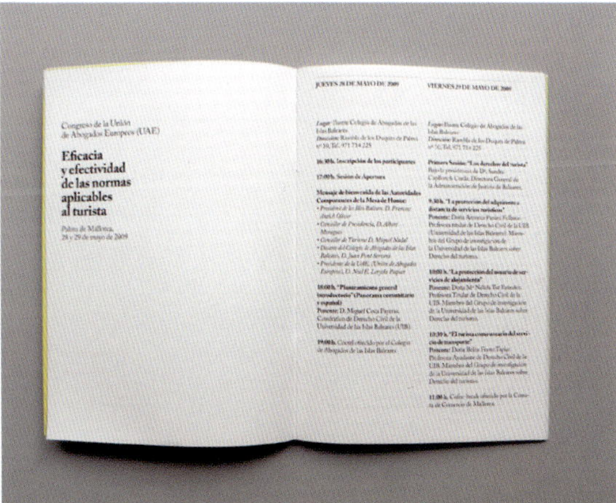
Congreso de la Unión
de Abogados Europeos (UAE)
Eficacia
y efectividad
de las normas
aplicables
al turista
Palma de Mallorca,
28 y 29 de mayo de 2009

ROCA JUNYENT
"la Caixa"
Presidència
de les Illes Balears
Govern de les Illes Balears

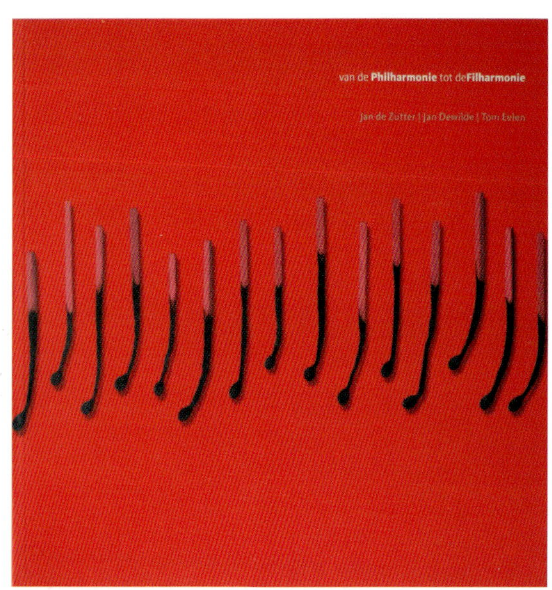

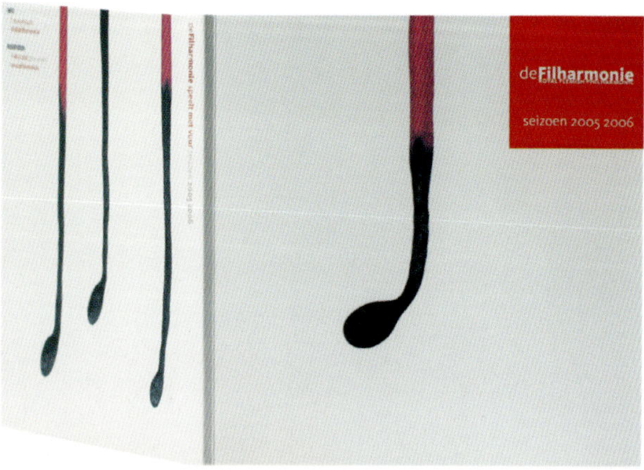

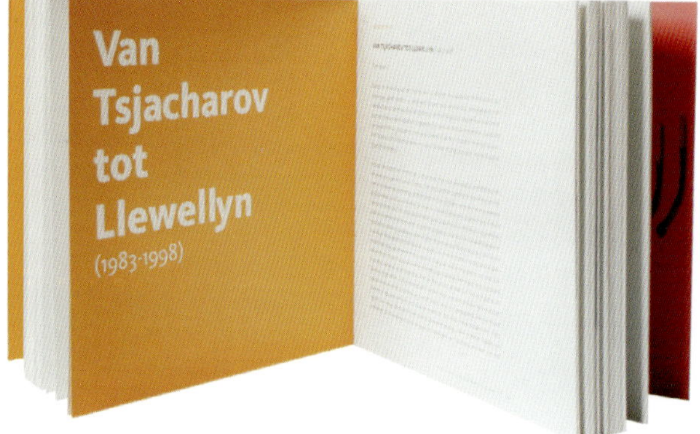

Gramma • *Concert series catalogue*

067/
Sonsoles Llorens • *Pamphlets presenting selected works of the studio*

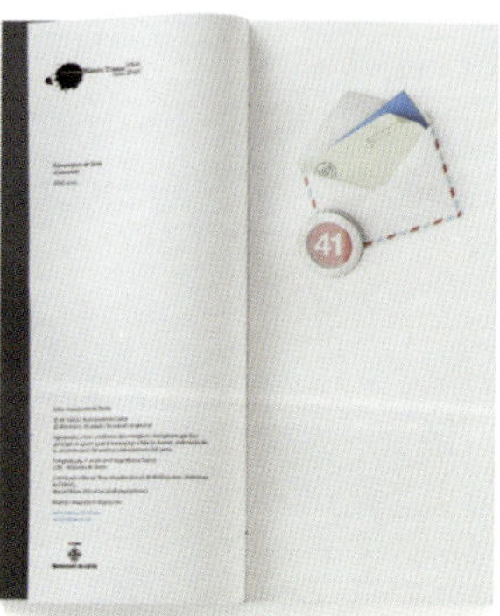

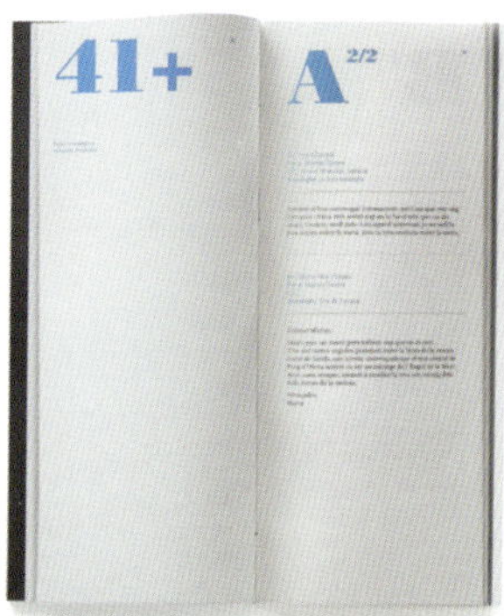

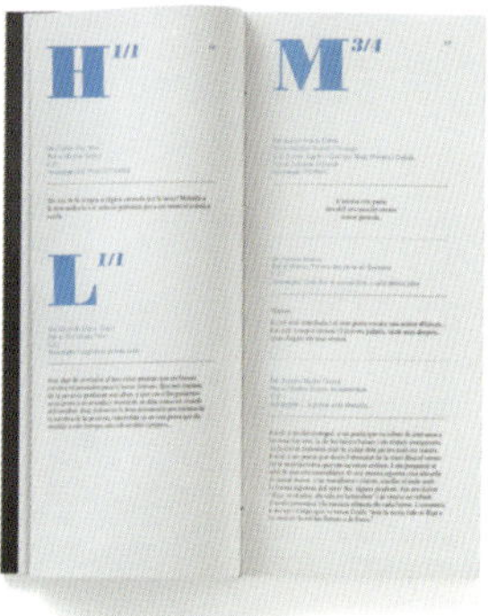

068/
ATIPUS • *Compilation of fictitious e-mails sent as tribute to the Catalan poet Marius Torres*

069/
Sonsoles Llorens • *Brochures presenting selected works of the studio*

070/
Paragon Marketing Communications • *Corporate profile for an Oman-based investment company*

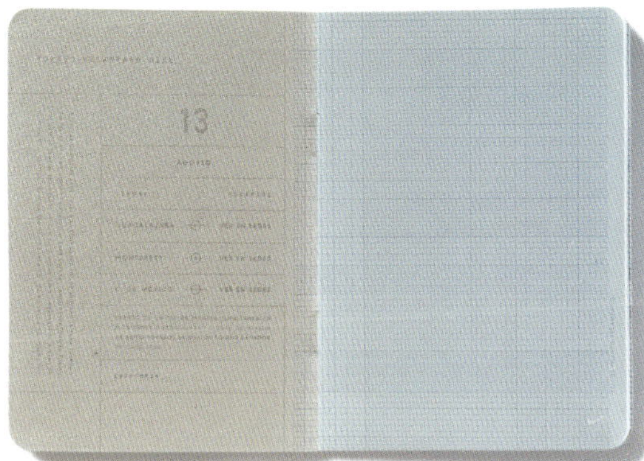

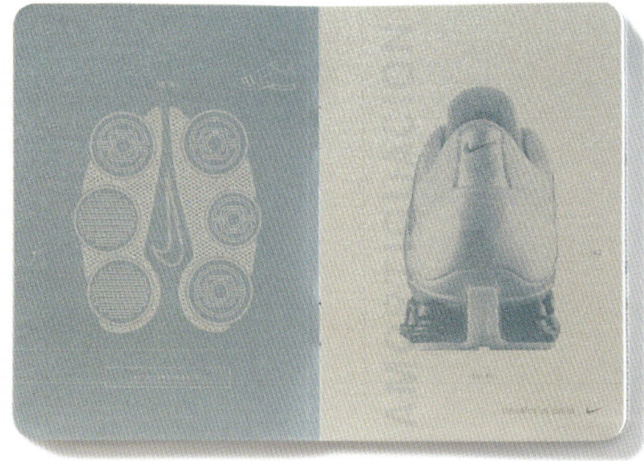

071/
Blok Design • *Booklet designed to inform the Nike consumer of events taking place and products being launched, thus cultivating consumer loyalty*

Whitenoise Design Limited • *Report examining the cultural landscape of Belfast*

1. STRATEGIC LEADERSHIP

STRATEGIC AIMS & OBJECTIVES

SHARED AREAS OF WORK

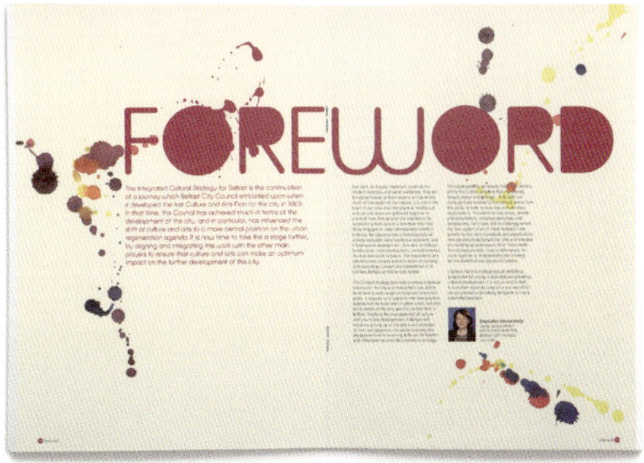

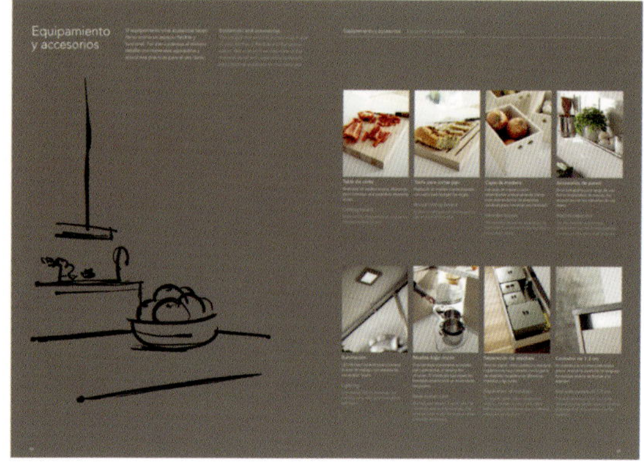

073/
Alambre Estudio • *Promotional leaflet designed for Serie 45, a new collection of kitchen designs and models*

074/
hazmecaso • *Catalogue describing the concerts recorded April 29 in Valencia, Alicante and Castellón*

075/
Pau Lamuà • *Typespecimen for typography 1M2, created exclusively for the exhibition project 1M2: Invasión Sutil*

AB
CD
EF
GH
IJ
KL
CON
XIT
ACO
NXI
TAC
ONX

076/
Diseño Cdroig • *Newspaper announcing real estate news, including tax exemptions and the sale and rental of housings*

077/
Neil Cutler Design • *Brochure announcing the special lunches and dinners during the celebrations of Christmas and New Year*

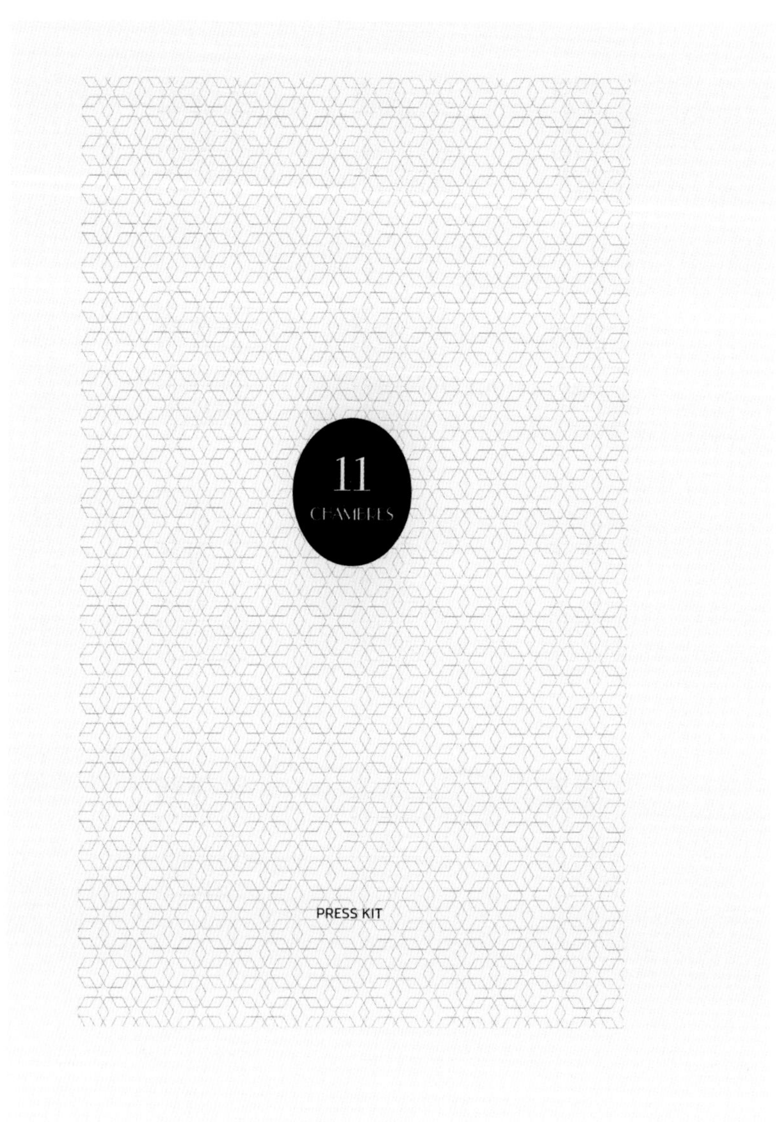

078/
Monsieur Mob • *Press kit for 11 chambres, a photography exhibition in Arles*

03 / THE PHOTOGRAPHERS

ESTELLE RANCUREL

Estelle Rancurel est une photographe de mode reconnue à Paris depuis 2001. Sa première série avec le magazine *Tribeca* a été remarquée, dès cette année-là, Estelle a été sollicitée par des magazines de mode avec lesquels elle continue de travailler (*Tschalkart Mademoiselle, Miss Behave, Blackpool, Cosmopolitan, Milk, Wad, Flavor, Sofa, Spray, Standard*).
Estelle privilégie un travail d'équipe avec la même équipe de stylistes et de coiffeurs maquilleurs, ce qui lui assure un regard consistant, toujours vibrant et décalé.

Cette orientation se retrouve dans une lumière recherchée qui fait ressortir "la beauté vraie". Que ce soit la matière textile ou les grains de peau de ses mannequins, le vrai jaillit de ses photos.
Estelle défend l'idée d'un casting recherché qui contribue à ses images. Les directeurs artistiques des revues les plus créatives considèrent ses images à la fois comme très modernes et en même temps très réalistes. Estelle est aussi reconnue pour la qualité de sa direction des mannequins, ce qui lui permet de dégager son propre style photographique, moderne et vivant, soit, finalement, très contemporain.

03 / THE PHOTOGRAPHERS

HERVÉ PLUMET

Hervé Plumet fut l'un des directeurs artistiques les plus titrés et admirés de sa génération dans l'univers publicitaire. Désireux de travailler autrement les images et les messages, Hervé est devenu un photographe et un réalisateur remarqué pour dorénavant réaliser les images que hier il dirigeait. Hervé tire son inspiration d'un caractère fait d'humour, de mélancolie et d'influences non reniées, telle celle de Saul Leiter.

Le travail d'Hervé Plumet est fait d'un jeu minutieux entre ombre et lumière pour faire émerger le message graphique : ce qui est donné à voir. Chez Hervé, la lumière est avant tout le moyen de donner naissance à une atmosphère mélancolique pour transmettre de vives émotions. Il aime fixer en une seule photo, une scène isolée puis laisser au spectateur la liberté d'imaginer une intrigue. Son expérience auprès des plus grandes sociétés lui permet de travailler avec une remarquable continuité la transmission des messages et des émotions. Artiste moderne, Hervé Plumet participe régulièrement à des expositions (le MAC VAL en 2006) et a bénéficié de nombreuses éditions.

079/
Marisa Gallén • *28-page pamphlet printed in two colours that reviews the 20-year history of Amores Grup de Percussió*

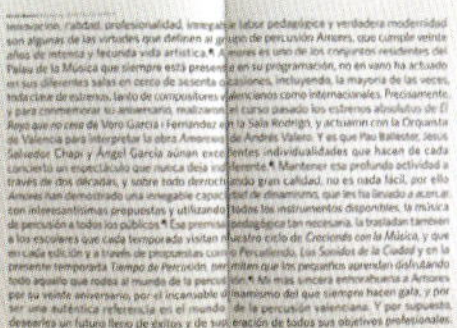

Innovación, calidad, profesionalidad, inmejorable labor pedagógica y verdadera modernidad son algunas de las virtudes que definen al grupo de percusión Amores, que cumple veinte años de intensa y fecunda vida artística.¶ Amores es uno de los conjuntos residentes del Palau de la Música que siempre está presente en su programación, no en vano ha actuado en sus diferentes salas en cerca de sesenta ocasiones, incluyendo, la mayoría de las veces, toda clase de estrenos, tanto de compositores valencianos como internacionales. Precisamente, y para conmemorar su aniversario, realizaron el curso pasado los estrenos absolutos de *El Rojo que no cesa* de Voro García i Fernández en la Sala Rodrigo, y actuaron con la Orquesta de Valencia para interpretar la obra *Amores* de Andrés Valero. Y es que Pau Ballester, Jesús Salvador Chapí y Ángel García aúnan excelentes individualidades que hacen de cada concierto un espectáculo que nunca deja indiferente.¶ Mantener esa profunda actividad a través de dos décadas, y sobre todo derrochando gran calidad, no es nada fácil, por ello Amores han demostrado una innegable capacidad de dinamismo, que les ha llevado a acercar con interesantísimas propuestas y utilizando todos los instrumentos disponibles, la música de percusión a todos los públicos.¶ Esa premisa pedagógica tan necesaria, la trasladan también a los escolares que cada temporada visitan nuestro ciclo de *Creciendo con la Música*, y que en cada edición y a través de propuestas como *Percutiendo*, *Los Sonidos de la Ciudad* y en la presente temporada *Tiempo de Percusión*, permiten que los pequeños aprendan disfrutando todo aquello que rodea al mundo de la percusión.¶ Mi más sincera enhorabuena a Amores por su veinte aniversario, por el incansable dinamismo del que siempre hacen gala, y por ser una auténtica referencia en el mundo de la percusión valenciana. Y por supuesto, desearles un futuro lleno de éxitos y de superación de todos sus objetivos profesionales.

080/
MusaWorkLab • *Book for Underconstruction Exhibition the artist Mónica de Miranda*

UNDER–
CONSTR
UCTION
PLATAFORMA /
PAUL
GOODWIN /
MANUELA
RIBEIRO SANCHEZ /
ARTERIA
ARCHITECTS /

HABITAR
E CONSTRUIR
NA "ZONA".
BUILDING
AND DWELLING
IN THE ZONE.
PAUL
GOODWIN –

UNDER–
CONSTR
UCTION
GREATER LISBON
UNDER–
CONSTR
UCTION
GREATER LISBON
PAUL
GOODWIN /
MÓNICA
DE MIRANDA

ÍNDICE /
CONTE
NTS.

081/
extra! • *Catalogue for Premi Medi Ambient, which promotes design for recycling products, projects and strategies*

PREMI
MEDI
2007
DISSENY
PER AL
RECICLATGE

Andorra és la soledat de les
muntanyes
i l'ambient de les
estacions d'esquí.

L'Andorre, c'est la solitude des montagnes
et l'ambiance des stations de ski.

Andorra té dues vides: a l'estiu, la de la calma a la natura; a l'hivern, la del domini esquiable més extens dels Pirineus.

Andorra és passejar i meditar, derrapar i anar a ballar.

Andorra té la calma i la tranquil·litat dels paisatges amplis, verges, nets, verds... buits. I el moviment de 281 quilòmetres d'ambient i de pistes, amb totes les instal·lacions i comoditats.

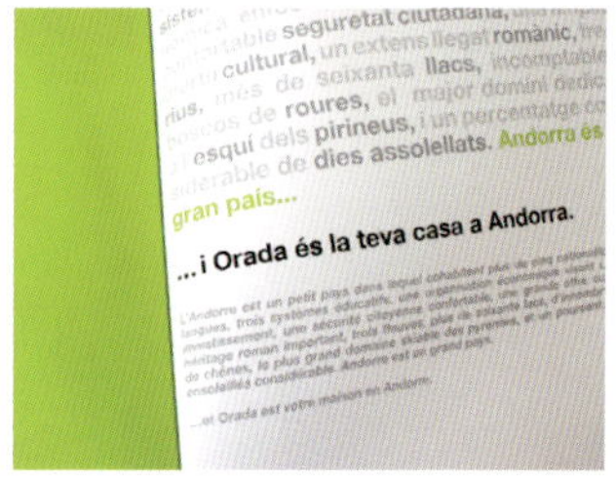

BAG.Disseny • *Brochure to position and to promote the benefits of buying real estate with Orada, a brokerage based in Andorra Orada*

083/
Doe de Do • *Brochure showcasing the menu of the restaurant eazie*

084/
Bisgràfic • *Catalogue promoting clothing to cribs and strollers*

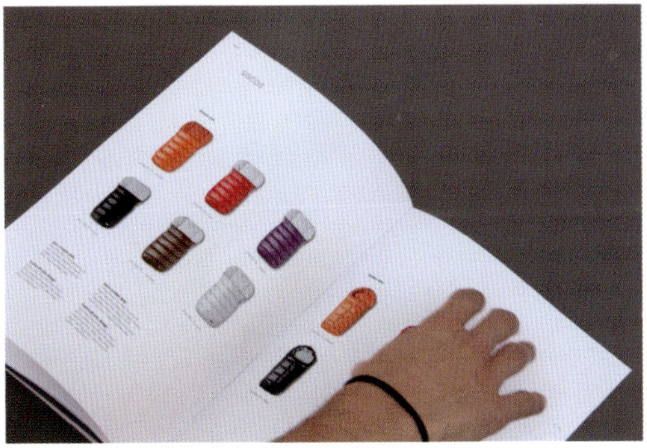

085/
Neil Cutler Design • *Brochure designed for the launch of Finca La Gramanosa extra virgin olive oil*

FINCA
LA GRAMANOSA

Finca La Gramanosa produce un exquisito acelte de oliva virgen extra, enmarcado dentro de la Denominación de Origen Siurana y elaborado a base de aceitunas arbequinas de primera calidad, procedentes de las mejores olivas arbequinas de nuestras propias tierras en la provincia de Tarragona y el municipio de Avinyonet.

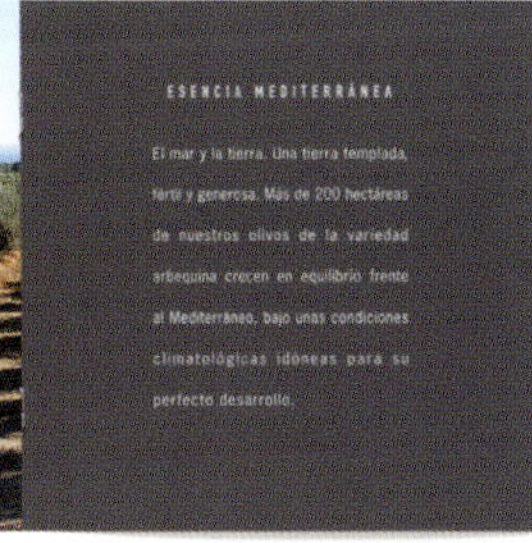

La búsqueda de la excelencia da como resultado un aceite de oliva de gran sabor.

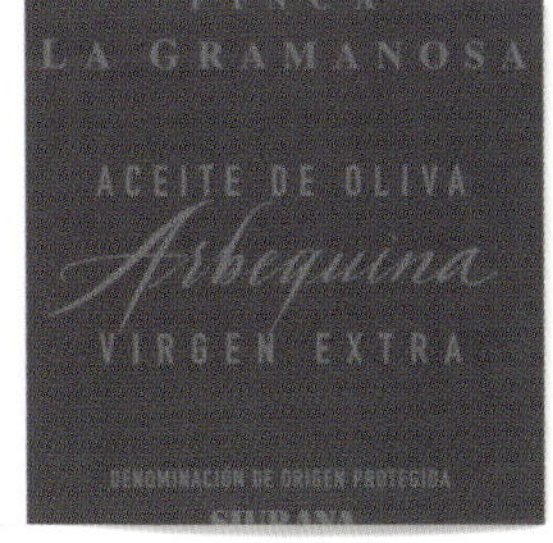

Duo Design • *Catalogue for Toilitech, a designer and manufacturer of public toilets*

La collection de choix
La gamme la plus large
et personnalisable

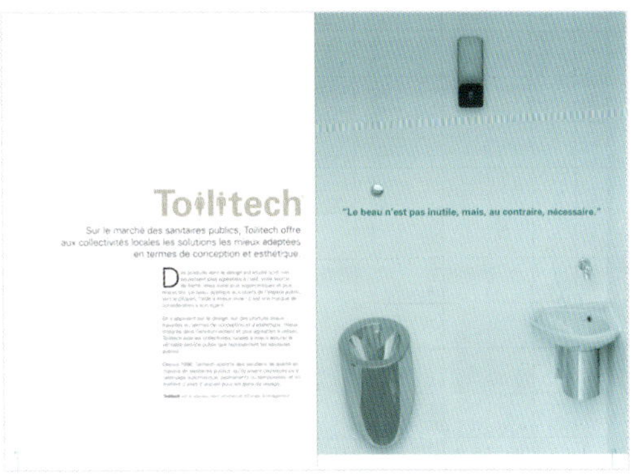
Toilitech
Sur le marché des sanitaires publics, Toilitech offre
aux collectivités locales les solutions les mieux adaptées
en termes de conception et esthétique
"Le beau n'est pas inutile, mais, au contraire, nécessaire."

Toilitech
La gamme la plus large
et personnalisable

Toilitech
Habiller et aménager

087/
La Camorra • *Pamphlet encouraging artists to enter the contest to create an icon representing the concept of innovation*

088/
Hyperakt • *Brochure explaining the amenities loft_2c has to offer*

089/
FK Design srl • *Catalogue for Dalla Costa pasta products*

Squisitezze Mare & Monti
I Formati
I Giganti Buoni
Dalla Costa
FUSILLONI
Specialità Tricolori
Profilo Aziendale
Passione per la qualità
Passion and quality
Seasonal Pasta
Kids Line
Gift Pasta & Licensing

090/
Cubo Diseño • *Advertising campaign for Tolosana, a bakery and catering company*

Como entrante:
1 • Mezcla de hojas verdes (canónigos, lechuga, ...)
2 • Aliñar con vinagre balsámico y aceite de oliva.
3 • Colocar la tarta de queso y miel.
Para servir como entrante en salsa o ensalada, o como guarnición en un primero.
Como plato principal:

• www.tolosana.com •

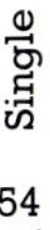

091/
extra! • *Forum programme detailing the use of fresh foods in modern cuisine*

Les cuines interactives:
cuina i tast

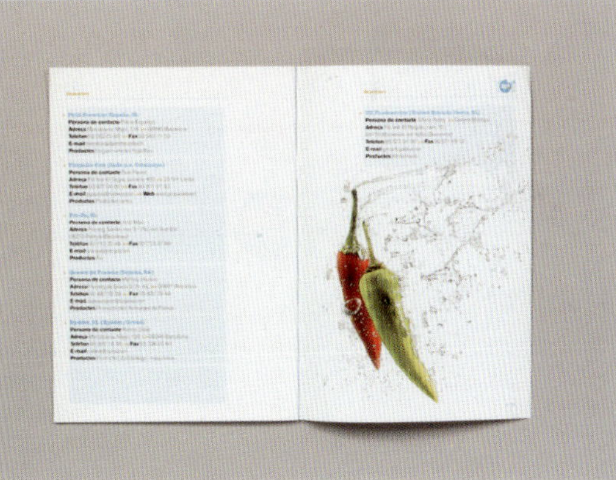

092/
VIS-TEK • *Catalogue/pamphlet explaining the corporate profile, products and solutions of Torre Agbar*

A different vision that looks to the future
Un regard différent vers le futur

The icon of a modern Barcelona
L'emblème de la Barcelone moderne

02.
Style
Style

093/
Signum Comunicación y Diseño, S.L. • *Brochure promoting real estate sales and investment opportunities*

094/
MusaWorkLab • *Postcard booklet for Bombay Sapphire printed on both high-gloss and matte papers*

EMBAL
AGEM
ÚNICA.

Cocktail
SAPPHIRE
DRY MARTINI
BOMBAY SAPPHIRE

095/
Eider Corral Estudio • *Catalogue presenting designer Aida Ulibarri's collection TRANSFORM during her scholarship of residence Bilbaoarte*

TRANSFORM
EMPTY YOUR MIND

TRANS
FORM
EMPTY
YOUR
MIND
02-X-09
20:05H

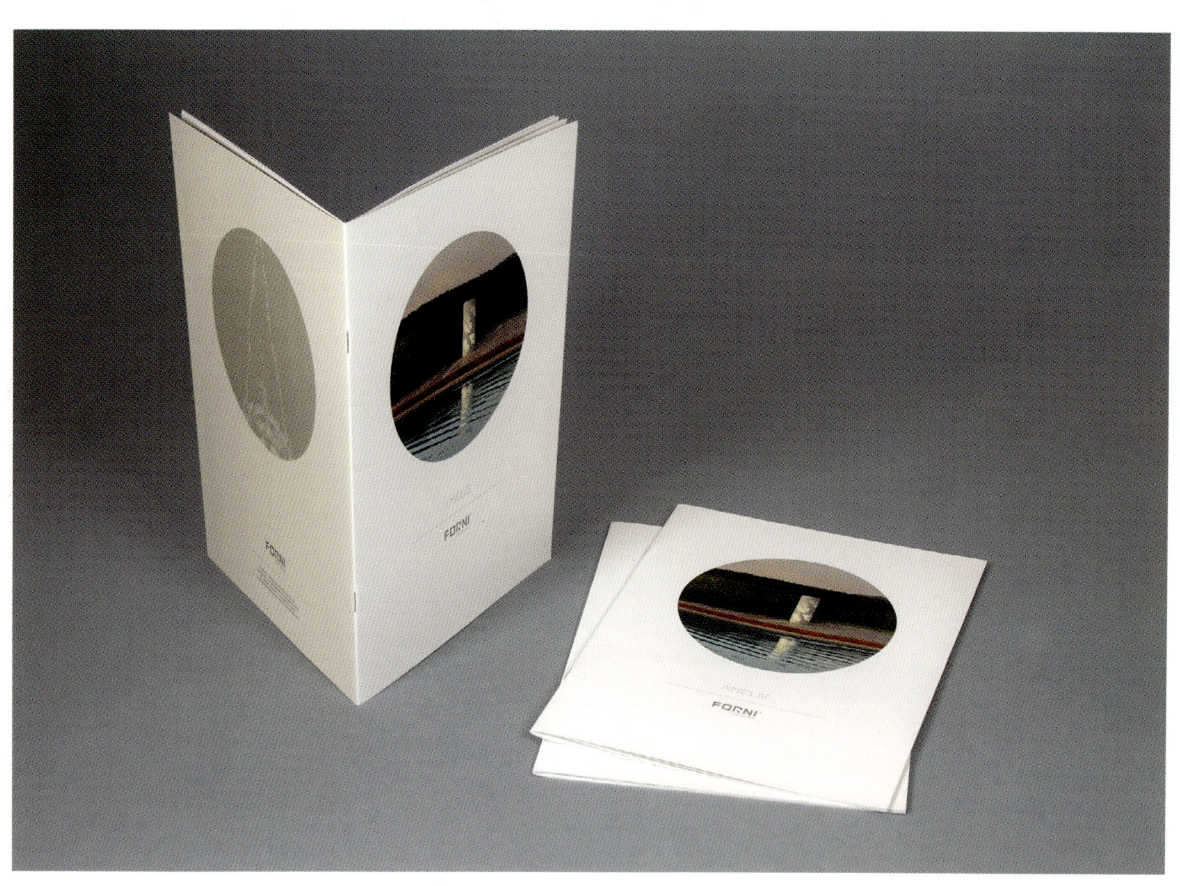

096/
studiosancisi • *Brochures to promote new product Amelie*

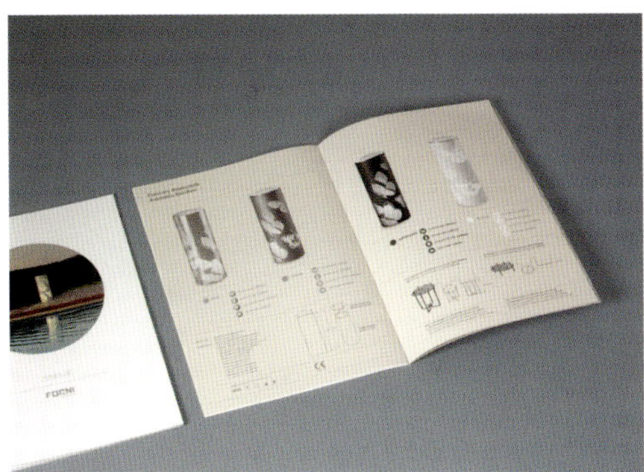

097/
MusaWorkLab • *Design report for Bombay Sapphire*

DESIGN
BOMBAY SAPPHIRE
INDEX REPORT

2
3
OS OUTROS
PREMIADOS

MUSA
BOMBAY

098/
Sonsoles Llorens • *Creation of a graphical identity for Voices of Peace, a program promoting reflection on the status of global violence*

DIUMENGE 7 DE SETEMBRE 2003. 18,30 H.

L'Auditori

PROGRAMA

MONTSE GUALLAR

AULA DE SO. COR INFANTIL SANT CUGAT
I nosaltres què? Els infants reivindiquem la nostra veu

LILIANA MAFFIOTTE
Piano

FEDERICO MAYOR ZARAGOZA
President de la Fundación Cultura de Paz

MARIONA SEGARRA
Cançó

JUAN MANUEL SUÁREZ DEL TORO
President Internacional de Creu Roja

LANÒNIMA IMPERIAL + GILDA OSWALDO CRUZ
Dansa i piano

FRANCISCO GONZÁLEZ BUENO
President d'Unicef - Comitè Espanyol

EULÀLIA SOLÉ
Piano

DADI JANKI
Co-directora Internacional Brahma Kumaris World Spiritual University. Guardiana de la Saviesa. Cimera de la Tierra

PROGRAMA

MONTSE GUALLAR

AULA DE SO. COR INFANTIL SANT CUGAT
¿Y nosotros qué? Los niños y niñas reivindicamos nuestra voz

LILIANA MAFFIOTTE
Piano

FEDERICO MAYOR ZARAGOZA
Presidente de la Fundación Cultura de Paz

MARIONA SEGARRA
Canción

JUAN MANUEL SUÁREZ DEL TORO
Presidente Internacional de Cruz Roja

LANÒNIMA IMPERIAL + GILDA OSWALDO CRUZ
Danza y piano

FRANCISCO GONZÁLEZ BUENO
Presidente de Unicef Comité Español

EULALIA SOLÉ
Piano

DADI JANKI
Co-directora Internacional Brahma Kumaris World Spiritual University. Guardiana de la Sabiduría. Cumbre de la Tierra

Cada vegada més, descobriments científics demostren la importància del període prenatal; en el que l'ésser humà construeix les bases de la seva salut, de la seva efectivitat, de les seves capacitats d'aprendre i de relacionar-se amb els altres. I ho fa en mig dels materials físics i psicològics aportats per la seva mare: tot el que viu la mare, el futur bebè també ho viu juntament amb ella. La mare, amb els seus pensaments, els seus sentiments, la seva forma de viure, els seus estats interiors, el va modelant. La mare, doncs, pot "educar" el nen o nena abans que neixi, entenent aquí per educació la capacitat de despertar, de desenvolupar totes les capacitats latents en l'individu, siguin aquestes d'ordre físic, emocional, intel·lectual, moral o espiritual.

Fer atenció al període prenatal és una forma de prevenció molt eficaç, ja que no només evita algunes deficiències i problemes (personals i socials) sinó que intervé en la formació de la salut física i psíquica de l'individu. És, doncs, una manera eficaç de prevenció de la violència, i contribueix de manera decisiva en la construcció de la cultura de la pau.

Cada vez más descubrimientos científicos demuestran la importancia del periodo prenatal. En él, el ser humano construye las primeras bases de su salud, de su afectividad, de sus capacidades de aprender y de relacionarse con los demás. Y lo hace en medio de los materiales físicos y psicológicos aportados por su madre. Todo lo que vive la madre, el futuro bebé también lo vive con ella. La madre, con sus pensamientos, sus sentimientos, su forma de vivir, sus estados interiores, le va modelando. La madre, pues, puede "educar" al niño/a antes de que éste nazca, entendiendo aquí por educación la capacidad de despertar, de desarrollar todas las capacidades latentes en el individuo, ya sean de orden físico, emocional, intelectual, moral o espiritual.

Prestar atención al periodo prenatal es una forma de prevención muy eficaz, puesto que no sólo evita ciertas deficiencias y ciertos problemas (de índole personal y social) sino que interviene en la formación de la salud física y psíquica del individuo. Es, pues, una forma eficaz de prevención de la violencia, y contribuye de manera decisiva a la construcción de la cultura de paz.

Avui, les estructures de guerra i dominació (sobre les persones, sobre les cultures, sobre els sistemes naturals) estan fermament atrinxerades. Però inevitablement canviaran, de la mateixa manera que tot canvia. Amb la consideració que cada ésser (sigui humà o no humà) té un valor inherent i que no pot ser posat en cap rànquing de jerarquies, ni comparat amb el valor d'un altre ésser, i amb la consideració que el sagrat no és fora d'aquest món, sinó que és manifesta en la natura, en els éssers humans, en la comunitat, en la cultura que anem creant, és possible anar assentant les bases d'un món lliure i just per a tothom, que permeti una vida sostenible per a cadascú, en el marc d'un medi natural i social també sostenibles. I hem d'esdevenir agents d'aquesta transformació ajudant a fer néixer un nou món, en Pau amb la Natura i en Pau amb les Cultures.

Hoy, las estructuras de guerra y dominación (sobre las personas, sobre las culturas, sobre los sistemas naturales) están firmemente atrincheradas. Pero inevitablemente cambiarán de la misma manera que todo cambia. Con la consideración de que cada ser (sea humano o no humano) tiene un valor inherente y que no se le puede colocar en ningún ranking de jerarquías, ni compararlo con el valor de otro ser, y con la consideración que lo sagrado no está fuera de este mundo sino que se manifiesta en la naturaleza, en los seres humanos, en la comunidad, en la cultura que vamos creando, es posible ir asentando las bases de un mundo libre y justo para todos. Que permita una vida sostenible para todos, en el marco de un medio natural y social también sostenible. Nos tenemos que convertir en agentes de esta transformación ayudando a nacer a un mundo nuevo, en Paz con la naturaleza y en Paz con las Culturas.

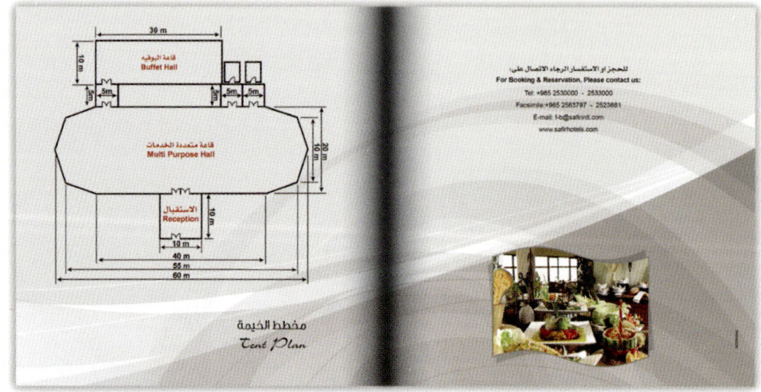

099/
Paragon Marketing Communications • *A small brochure for a famous hotel in Kuwait*

100/
Sonsoles Llorens • *Brochure for Fòrum Universal de les Cultures 2004*

101/
Keith Kitz • *Promotional brochure describing CBS Personnel Holdings, Inc. and its mergers and acquisitions*

102/
Quattro idcp • *Illustrated manual of telecommunications services*

103/
FullblastCreative.com • *Custom brochure with 140-lb. cover stock with 12-page brochure inside and bound with aluminum grommets*

BIOSCIENCE
Welcome to Waggener Edstrom Bioscience

AREAS OF EXPERTISE
COMMUNICATIONS DISCIPLINES

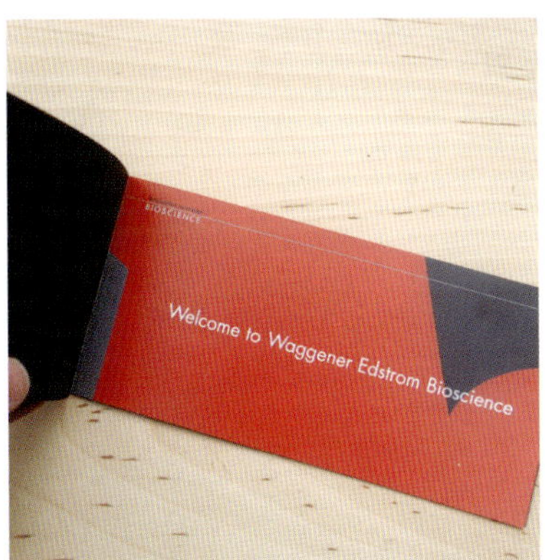
BIOSCIENCE
Welcome to Waggener Edstrom Bioscience

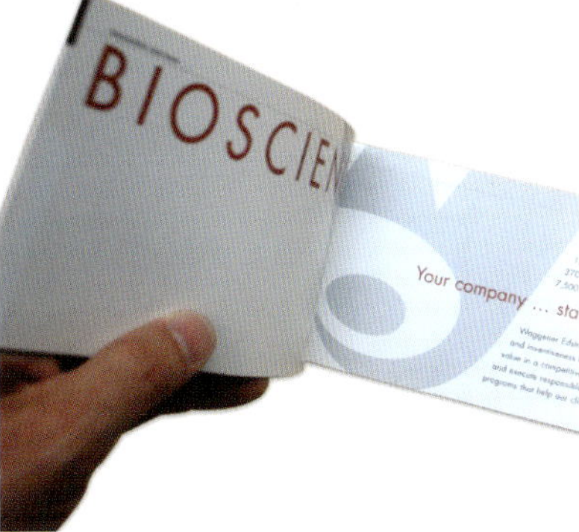
Your company

StudioCentro Marketing • *Brochure including calendar and posters to celebrate the New Year and to promote R&C Lab*

PER VOI UNA SICUREZZA COMPETITIVA
IL CONTATTO È SEMPRE APERTO
SCEGLIETE VOI QUANDO
R&C LAB SRL
Via Retrone 29/31
36077 Altavilla Vicentina VI
telefono 0444.349040 · fax 0444.349041
rc@rclabsrl.it
sede di TORINO
Via Orbassano 98 · 10090 Bruino · TO
telefono 0119085188 · Fax: 0119087943
rc.torino@rclabsrl.it
sede di MILANO
Via Verro 33/6 · Milano
telefono 02 89550352 · fax 02 89550352
sede di TRENTO
Via Catoni 15 · Loc. Mattarello · Trento
telefono 0461942315 · fax 0461942315
sede di CATANIA
Via VIII Strada 8 - Z.I. · Catania
telefono 0957357676 · fax 0957351890
rc.catania@rclabsrl.it

PUNTI DI RIFERIMENTO
PRESERVARE LE RISORSE AMBIENTALI E CULTURALI

PRESENTATECI LE VOSTRE ESIGENZE
AL CENTRO DI TUTTO LE PERSONE

CONSULTA VIA WEB LA SITUAZIONE DEI CAMPIONI E I RISULTATI
RISPOSTE SICURE
SCELTE SICURE

001/ - Brochure number
lila&tom / Anna Farré - Studio name
La Compagnie des Petits - Client name
Spain - Country

Children's Fashion Collection 2010-2011
for La Compagnie des Petits - Brochure description

014/
Fons Hickmann m23
Grafic Europe
Germany

Exhibition brochure for Grafic Europe

015/
BURO-GDS
BURO-GDS
United States (USA)

I AM YOU, a book by Ellen Zhao, examines the relationship between the book and the reader

016/
MusaWorkLab
Centrocar
Portugal

Brochure presenting the corporate values of Centrocar in a very contemporary way

017/
ATIPUS
Celler el Masroig
Spain

Celler el Masroig winery catalogue, which incorporates product sheets that can be removed and inserted

018/
Kanella
Dr. Yiannis Vamvakaris / Femina
Greece

Three brochures for the three phases of pregnancy; the front cover of each brochure series has a unique die-cut that is inspired by the changing shape of a woman's body in each phase of pregnancy

019/
Fernandez Alvarez®
Embo
Spain

Catalogue of light covers for aluminum structure

020/
SOGOOD
VMS Veiligheidsprogramma (VMS Safety Program)
Netherlands

Brochure series that put patient safety first. Explaining how the medical staff in hospitals, dealing with different illnesses, can prevent making mistakes, in a simple, clear and sympathetic way

021/
Sonsoles Llorens
Álvaro Gómez-Jordana
Spain

Brochure-offprint for the newspaper La Vanguardia

022/
rumorvisual
Patronato de Turismo de Cáceres
Spain

Brochure series promoting tourism in the province of Cáceres

023/
David Torrents
Krtu
Spain

Flyers for Gràfiques Ocultes, a graphic design exhibition

024/
David Torrents
Krtu
Spain

Flyers for an exhibition of contemporary circus

025/
Murray agencia de diseño
Ayuntamiento de San Sebastián de los Reyes
Spain

Monthly cultural agenda

026/
Oxigen comunicació gràfica
Casal Lambda
Spain

Agendas printed in one colour and black

027/
Sonsoles Llorens
Escofet
Spain

Collection of pamphlets highlighting the artistry of Escofet products

028/
Dúctil
Ajuntament de Sant Lluís
Spain

2007-2008 catalogue of Christmas and New Year festivals

029/
BATLLEGROUP
BAU ESCOLA SUPERIOR DE DISSENY
Spain

An array of design study catalogues.

030/
Bisgràfic
Monens
Spain

Catalogue of children's furniture that is singular for its aesthetic lines and color notes

031/
Sonsoles Llorens
Tecla Sala
Spain

A pop-art rendering of "Union Jack" conveys an atmosphere of vanguard for this exhibition on the new generation of contemporary British artists

032/
Villuendas+Gómez Disseny
El Prat ràdio
Spain

Promotional and informative pamphlet that outlines programming of the radio station

033/
elDiseñador s.c.p
Le Merídien Hotels Barcelona
Spain

Flyers for Le Merídien Barcelona, Le POPBAR

034/
BENBENWORLD
Le Vivat (Theater)
Belgium

2010-2011 season catalogue for the theatre Le Vivat

035/
Whitenoise Design Limited
Belfast City Council
United Kingdom

Brochure documenting art that connects the communities of Belfast

036/
Dandelion
Martindale Pharma
United Kingdom

Brochure explaining the rebrand of Martindale Pharma®

037/
Hoet&Hoet
Maries's Corner
Belgium

Catalogue for Marie's Corner.

038/
BENBENWORLD
Le Vivat (Theater)
Belgium

Leaflet. detailing the 20-year anniversary of the theatre Le Vivat

039/
Murray agencia de diseño
Mustang
Spain

Brochure promoting Mustang's campaign autumn winter 2008

040/
Barfutura
Alta Films
Spain

Pressbook for the film La Isla Interior by Félix Sabroso and Dunia Ayaso

041/
Nifava + Canseixanta
Ajuntament de Banyoles
Spain

Design and layout explaining the photo-romance Ramoneta, which was incorporated into the programme of the Banyoles Municipal Theatre of Performing Arts

042/
Whitenoise Design Limited
ORANGE
United Kingdom

Illustrated brochure for the 2005 corporate responsibility report for Orange UK

043/
La Camorra
FECYT
Spain

Pamphlet for a 2009 conference organised by la Fundación Española para la Ciencia y la Tecnología (FECYT) and Institute Cervantes

044/
seesponge
Yarema Marquetry
United States (USA)

Catalogue and sales tool of the product line of Yarema Marquetry, a designer and manufacturer of semi-custom wood inlays

045/
extra!
Col·legi d'Ambientòlegs de Catalunya (COAMB)
Spain

Corporate brochure and annual report

046/
Whitenoise Design Limited
TASC
United Kingdom

Brochure design for the H.E.A.P. Chart - a hierarchy of earnings, attributes and privilege analysis

047/
FK Design srl
Fabbian illuminazione Spa
Italy

General catalogue Fabbian Illuminazione

048/
Toormix
Toormix
Spain

Publication-type portfolio with a selection of the most recent projects of the studio

049/
neura projectes
Laipals
Spain

Promotional catalog

050/
BURO-GDS
ENSAD
United States (USA)

Booklet documenting the student exchange program participation by three schools in France and Thailand..

051/
Juan Martinez Estudio
Gráficas Vernetta
Spain

Promotional publication

052/
Xavier Martínez Balet
Fundación Taller de Guionistas (Productora RodaryRodar)
Spain

2008-09 programme for Fundación Taller de Guionistas

053/
2FRESH
ATU Duty Free
United Kingdom

Brochure for ATU honouring Frontier Awards

054/
Blok Design
Evolutiva
Mexico

Brochure designed in a book format for a company that specialises in leadership coaching

055/
Carol García del Busto
Universidad de Alcalá - Siece
Spain

Design for the 5th annual seminar on the history of the written word, hosted by Universidad de Alcalá

056/
Barfutura
MOD Producciones
Spain

Pressbook with 72 pages for the film El Mal Ajeno

057/
FK Design srl
H. Krull & C. Srl
Italy

Brochure promoting the line of shaving brushes from Acca Kappa

058/
oikos associati
cleaf
Italy

Promotional brochure for CLEAF, an Italy-based designer, manufacturer, and finisher of surfaces for interior design

059/
Logoorange Design Studio
Education International
Romania

40pages brochure for Education International, a global federation of teacher unions

060/
El vivero
Museo Nacional Centro de Arte Reina Sofía, Madrid
Spain

Pamphlet describing the Alia Syed exhibition at El Museo Nacional Centro de Arte Reina Sofía

061/
MusaWorkLab
Monica de Miranda Artist
Portugal

Catalogue for the Underconstruction exhibition from the artist Mónica de Miranda

062/
Logoorange Design Studio
Type R Magazine
Romania

Type R Magazine brochure

063/
Grupo Anton Comunicacion / 6 Sombreros Creativos / Diseño: Fuensanta Blanca
Torregrosa
Spain

Book presenting the of works of Torregrosa.

064/
Alambre Estudio
dica
Spain

Promotional catalogue for the new collection of VITA bath

065/
Dúctil
Unión de Abogados Europeos
Spain

Dossier that containing the proposal of activities and schedules for an international congress

066/
Gramma
de Filharmonie
Belgium

Concert series catalogue

067/
Sonsoles Llorens
Sonsoles Llorens. Estudi de disseny
Spain

Pamphlets presenting selected works of the studio

068/
ATIPUS
Ajuntament de Lleida
Spain

Compilation of fictitious e-mails sent as tribute to the Catalan poet Marius Torres

069/
Sonsoles Llorens
Sonsoles Llorens. Estudi de disseny
Spain

Brochures presenting selected works of the studio.

070/
Paragon Marketing Communications
Atyab investments
Kuwait

Corporate profile for an Oman-based investment company

071/
Blok Design
Nike
Mexico

Booklet designed to inform the Nike consumer of events taking place and products being launched, thus cultivating consumer loyalty

072/
Whitenoise Design Limited
Belfast City Council
United Kingdom

Report examining the cultural landscape of Belfast

073/
Alambre Estudio
dica
Spain

Promotional leaflet designed for Serie 45, a new collection of kitchen designs and models

074/
hazmecaso
IVM. Institut Valencià de la Música. Generalitat Valenciana
Spain

Catalogue describing the concerts recorded April 29 in Valencia, Alicante and Castellón

075/
Pau Lamuà
1M2 TYPESPECIMEN
Spain

Typespecimen for typography 1M2, created exclusively for the exhibition project 1M2: Invasión Sutil

076/
Diseño Cdroig
Primer Grupo Franquicias
Spain

Newspaper announcing real estate news, including tax exemptions and the sale and rental of housings

077/
Neil Cutler Design
Starman Hoteles España SL
Spain

Brochure announcing the special lunches and dinners during the celebrations of Christmas and New Year

078/
Monsieur Mob
Valerie Hersleven
France

Press kit for 11 chambres, a photography exhibition in Arles

079/
Marisa Gallén
Amores Grup de Pecussió
Spain

28-page pamphlet printed in two colours that reviews the 20-year history of Amores Grup de Percussió

080/
MusaWorkLab
Mónica de Miranda Artist
Portugal

Book for Underconstruction Exhibition the artist Mónica de Miranda

081/
extra!
Agència de Residus de Catalunya
Spain

Catalogue for Premi Medi Ambient, which promotes design for recycling products, projects and strategies

082/
BAG.Disseny
Orada
Andorra

Brochure to position and to promote the benefits of buying real estate with Orada, a brokerage based in Andorra Orada

083/
Doe de Do
eazie
Netherlands

Brochure showcasing the menu of the restaurant eazie

084/
Bisgràfic
Praia
Spain

Catalogue promoting clothing to cribs and strollers.

085/
Neil Cutler Design
Germina Fruit SL
Spain

Brochure designed for the launch of Finca La Gramanosa extra virgin olive oil

086/
Duo Design
Toilitech
France

Catalogue for Toilitech, a designer and manufacturer of public toilets

087/
La Camorra
FECYT
Spain

Pamphlet encouraging artists to enter the contest to create an icon representing the concept of innovation

088/
Hyperakt
loft_2c
United States

Brochure explaining the amenities loft_2c has to offer

089/
FK Design srl
Dalla Costa Alimentare Srl
Italy

Catalogue for Dalla Costa pasta products

090/
Cubo Diseño
TOLOSANA
Spain

Advertising campaign for Tolosana, a bakery and catering company.

091/
extra!
Mercabarna
Spain

Forum programme detailing the use of fresh foods in modern cuisine

092/
VIS-TEK
Grupo Agbar
Spain

Catalogue/pamphlet explaining the corporate profile, products and solutions of Torre Agbar

093/
Signum Comunicación y Diseño, S.L.
FIMASA
Spain

Brochure promoting real estate sales and investment opportunities

094/
MusaWorkLab
Bombay Sapphire
Portugal

Postcard booklet for Bombay Sapphire printed on both high-gloss and matte papers

095/
Eider Corral Estudio
Aida Ulibarri
Spain

Catalogue presenting designer Aida Ulibarri's collection TRANSFORM during her scholarship of residence Bilbaoarte.

096/
studiosancisi
Forni
Italy

Brochures to promote new product Amelie

097/
MusaWorkLab
Bombay Sapphire
Portugal

Design report for Bombay Sapphire

098/
Sonsoles Llorens
Brahma Kumaris Universidad Espiritual Mundial
Spain

Creation of a graphical identity for Voices of Peace, a program promoting reflection on the status of global violence

099/
Paragon Marketing Communications
Safir Hotels & Resorts
Kuwait

A small brochure for a famous hotel in Kuwait

100/
Sonsoles Llorens
Ajuntament de Barcelona
Spain

Brochure for Fòrum Universal de les Cultures 2004

101/
Keith Kitz
CBS Personnel Holdings, Inc
United States (USA)

Promotional brochure describing CBS Personnel Holdings, Inc. and its mergers and acquisitions

102/
Quattro idcp
R, cable y telecomunicaciones
Spain

Illustrated manual of telecommunications services

103/
FullblastCreative.com
Wagener Edstrom Worldwide
United States (USA)

Custom brochure with 140-lb. cover stock with 12-page brochure inside and bound with aluminum grommets

104/
StudioCentro Marketing
R&C Lab
Italy

Brochure including calendar and posters to celebrate the New Year and to promote R&C Lab

Multiple Folds

186 - 299

105/
ATIPUS • *Promotional catalogue detailing 10 years of strategic design from Atipus, including selected examples of the studio's work*

Serveis
Web
Serveis web
Gestió
i manteniment
Serveis web
Creació d'eines
específiques

MAS
DE DALT

Erretres Diseño • *Exhibition pamphlet*

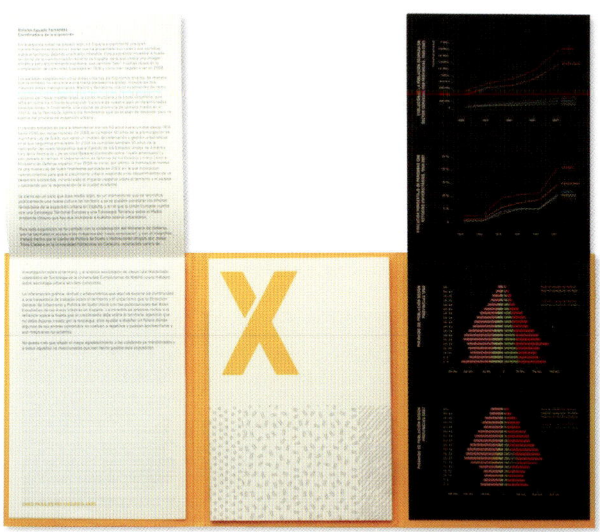

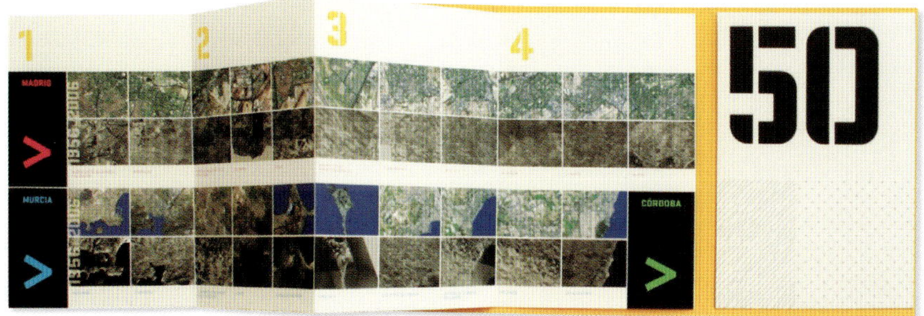
1
2
3
4
MADRID
MURCIA
CÓRDOBA
50

107/
Nifava • *Image of S de Saderra show, designed specifically as a tribute to the Catalan composer of sardanas Manel Saderra*

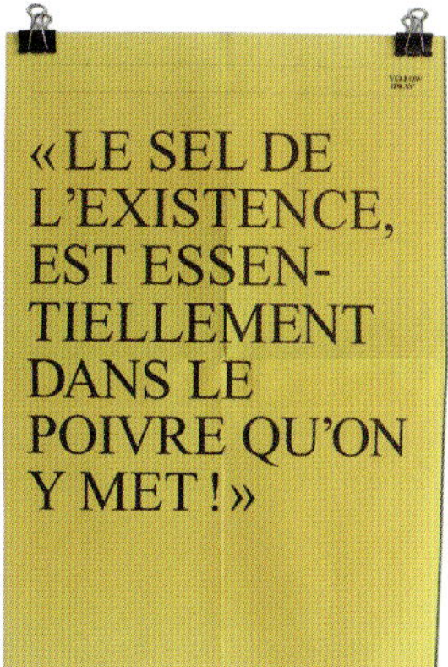

108/
Oxigen comunicació gràfica • *Fold-out pamphlet that details the different lectures and creativity seminars offered by Yellow Ideas*

109/
ENFÁTIKA • *Internal marketing campaign to encourage employees to submit ideas on how their company and workplace can be improved*

Recuerda,
buscamos
tus ideas.

rda,
mos
eas.

Recuerda,
buscamos
tus ideas.

Recuerda,
buscamos
tus ideas.
Tu aportación es esencial.
Participa con tus ideas para mejorar tu trabajo y el funcionamiento de la empresa en calidad, instalaciones, seguridad laboral, protección del medio ambiente, ahorro de tiempo y eliminación de gastos y de trámites innecesarios.
Tus ideas tienen premio. ¡Participa!

Recuerda,
buscamos
tus ideas.
Tu aportación es esencial.
Participa con tus ideas para mejorar tu trabajo y el funcionamiento de la empresa en calidad, instalaciones, seguridad laboral, protección del medio ambiente, ahorro de tiempo y eliminación de gastos y de trámites innecesarios.
Tus ideas tienen premio. ¡Participa!

Todo lo
que es
posible
se puede
conseguir

Todo lo
que es
posible
se puede
conseguir

Todo lo
que es
posible
se puede
conseguir
Premios
Idea del año

Todo lo
que es
posible
se puede
conseguir

Multiple Folds

194
/
195

110/
Diseño Cdroig • *Prestigious graphic design pamphlet*

EM
PRE
SA
PRO
YEC
TOS

PRO
YEC
TOS

EM
PRE
SA

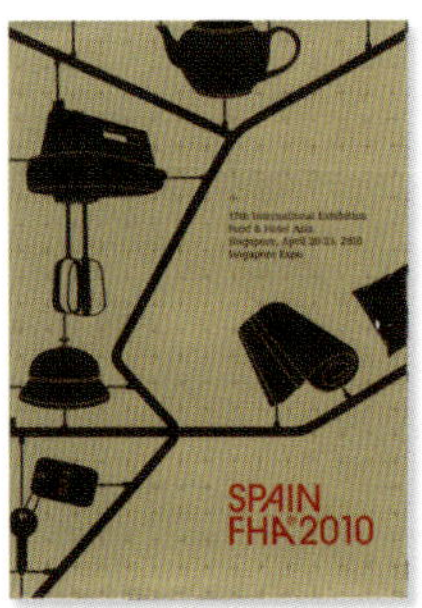

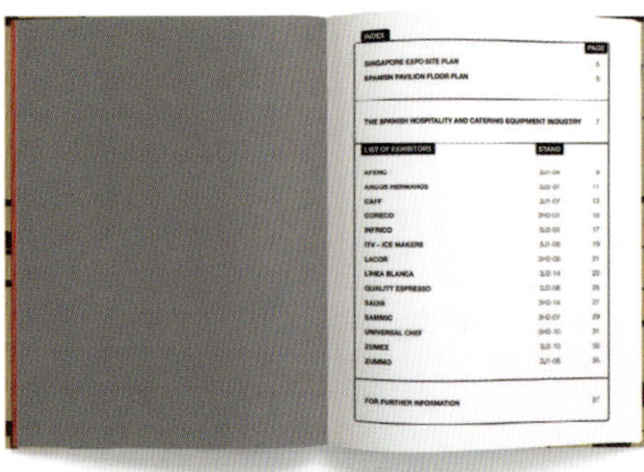

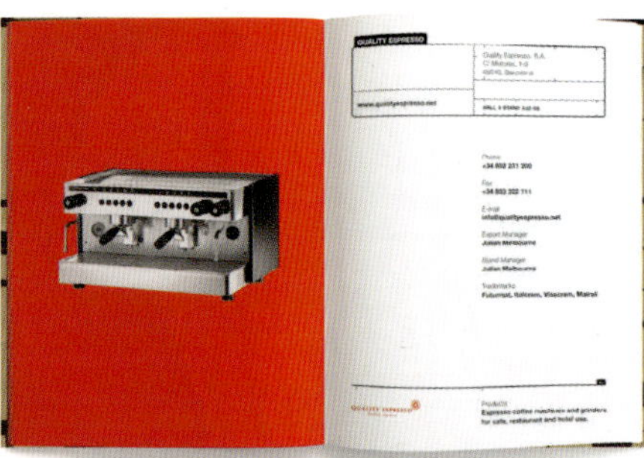

111/
Erretres Diseño • *Pamphlet designed for FHA2010, an international food and hospitality trade exposition held in Singapore*

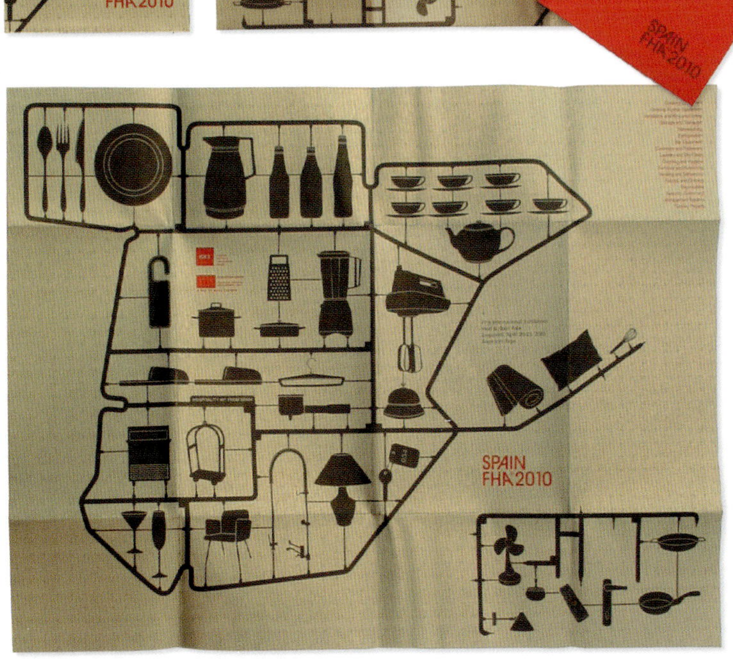
SPAIN
FHA 2010

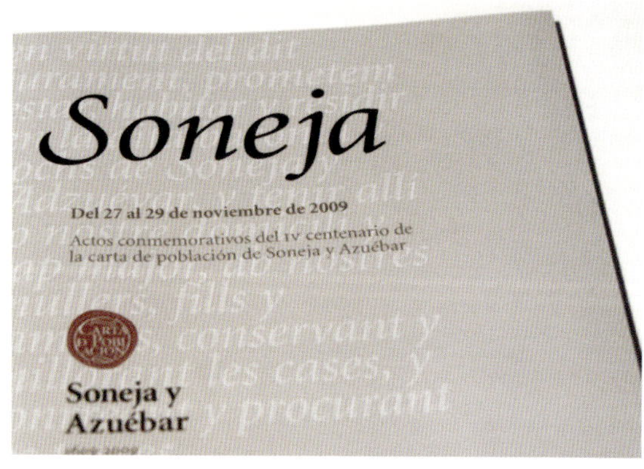

112/
Ideario Chinín • *Pamphlet highlighting the programme of commemorative acts in recognition of the 400th anniversary of the charter of the town Soneja*

113/
Blok Design • *Visitors' guide brochure for El Zanjón, historic building in Buenos Aires*

114/
Cubo Diseño • *Press dossier for Dinópolis, a dinosaur theme park, which was distributed during the international exposition of Zaragoza*

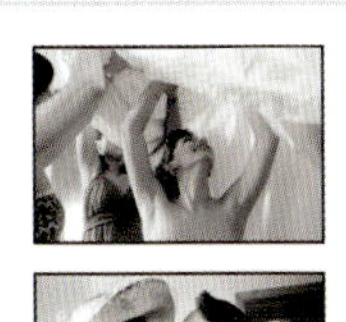

115/
CADG • *Pamphlet for photography studio*

116/
oikos associati • *Fold-out brochure for DecorTile, a product line from OmniDecor®*

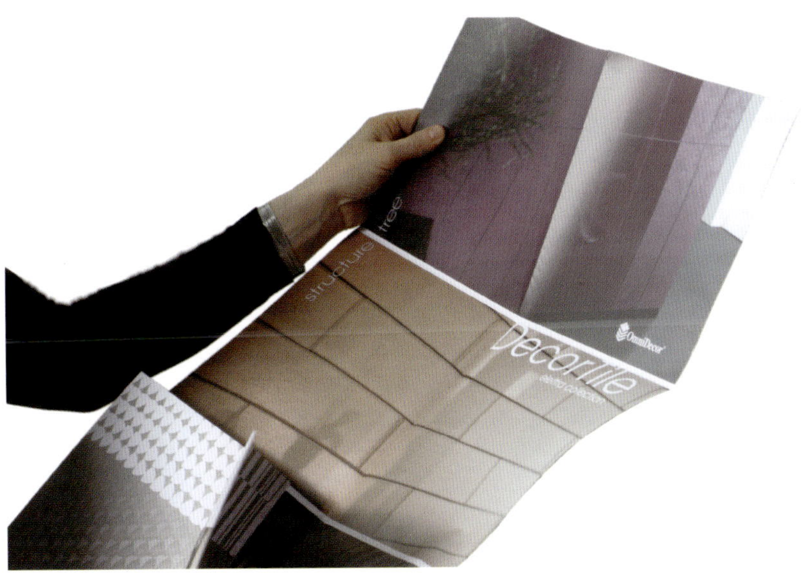
structure tree
Decortile
OmniDecor

Decortile
elettra collection
OmniDecor

117/
Nifava • *Accordion-fold brochure promoting a film series on issues related to social inclusion*

118/
ENFÁTIKA • *Programme of the Certamen Contest*

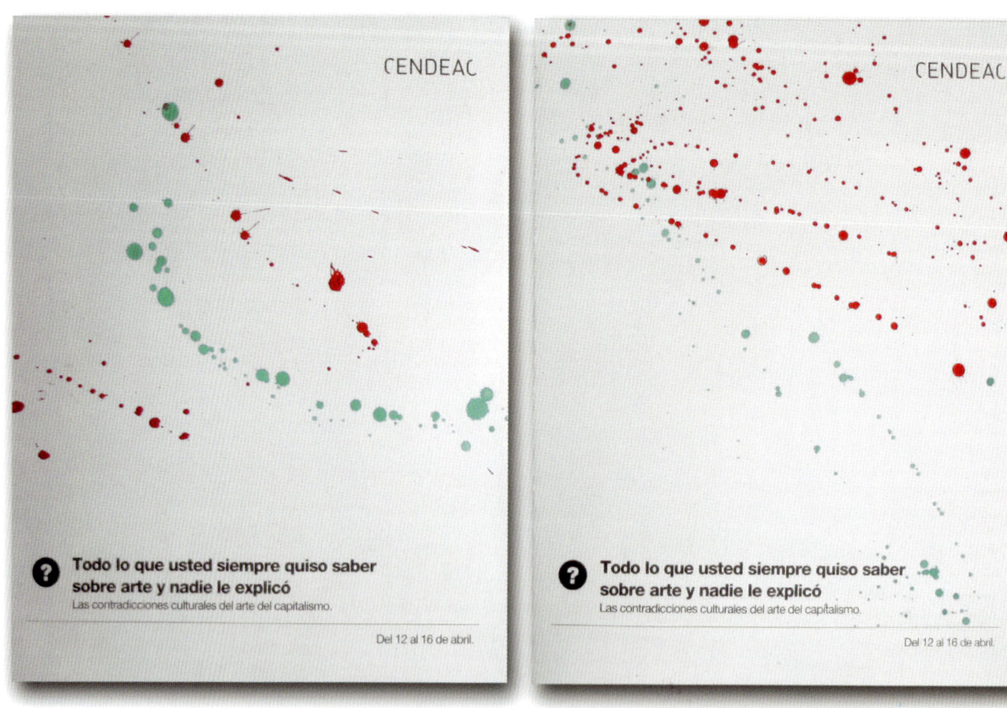

119/
Sublima Comunicación • *Pamphlet for the new course from Centro de Documentación y Estudios Avanzados de Arte Contemporáneo (CENDEAC)*

Este curso pretende proporcionar, tanto a un público no iniciado como a los aficionados no especialistas, recursos suficientes para acercarse con espíritu crítico al arte contemporáneo y al contexto cultural en el que surge. A partir del comentario de las imágenes más significativas del arte de los últimos 50 años discutirá las razones por las que han adquirido esa consideración de privilegio en su contexto sociocultural, sin simplificarlas pero sin complicarlas.

Programa
Este curso constará de seis temas impartidos en cinco sesiones

Información adicional

Ficha de inscripción

"Todo lo que usted siempre quiso saber sobre arte y nadie le explicó" o Las contradicciones culturales del arte del capitalismo.

Curso de introducción al arte contemporáneo, impartido por Ramón Salas.

Del 12 al 16 de abril.
18.00 h.

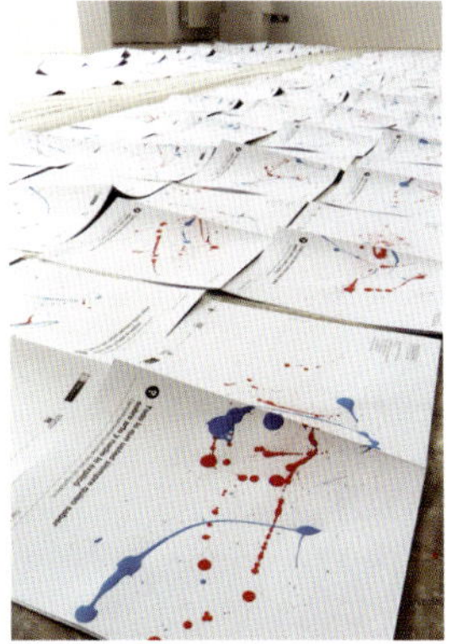

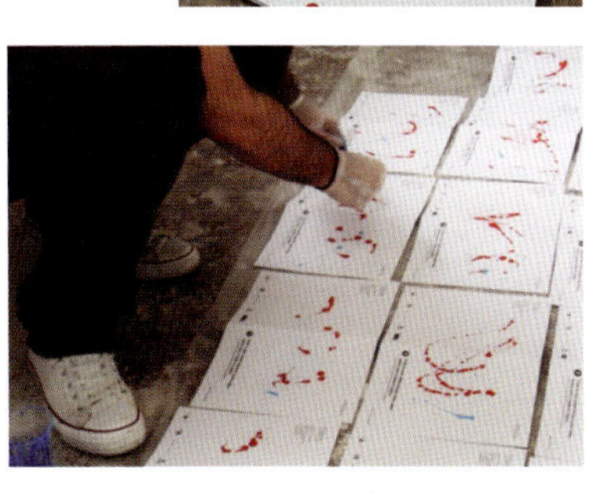

120/
Thonik • *Design of the corporate identity and campaign to mark the 25th anniversary of the Tokyo art institution, Spiral*

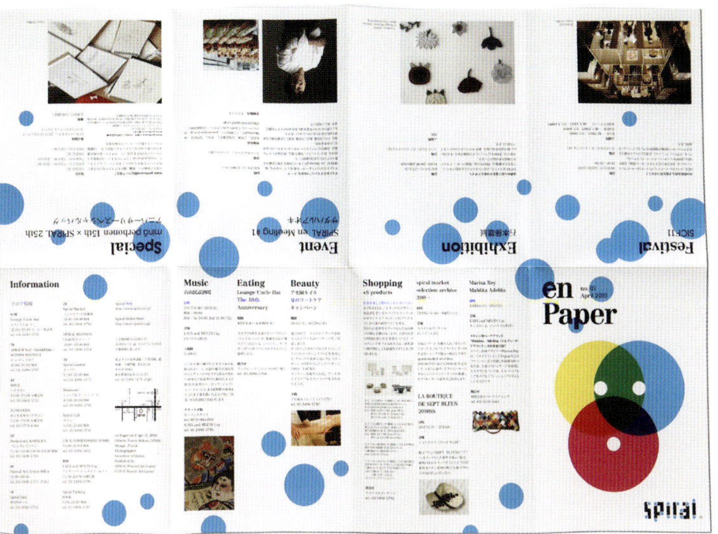
Special
mina perhonen 15th × SPIRAL 25th
Event
Exhibition
Festival
Information
Music
Eating
Beauty
Shopping
en Paper
no. 01
April 2010

en Paper
no. 01
April 2010
Event
Special
mina perhonen 15th × SPIRAL 25th
アニバーサリースペシャルバッグ

121/
Miller Meiers Design for Communication • *Introductory brochure explaining the services of One Point Security Solutions*

122/
dot. • *Pamphlet daily programmes of an entrepreneur in Andalusia*

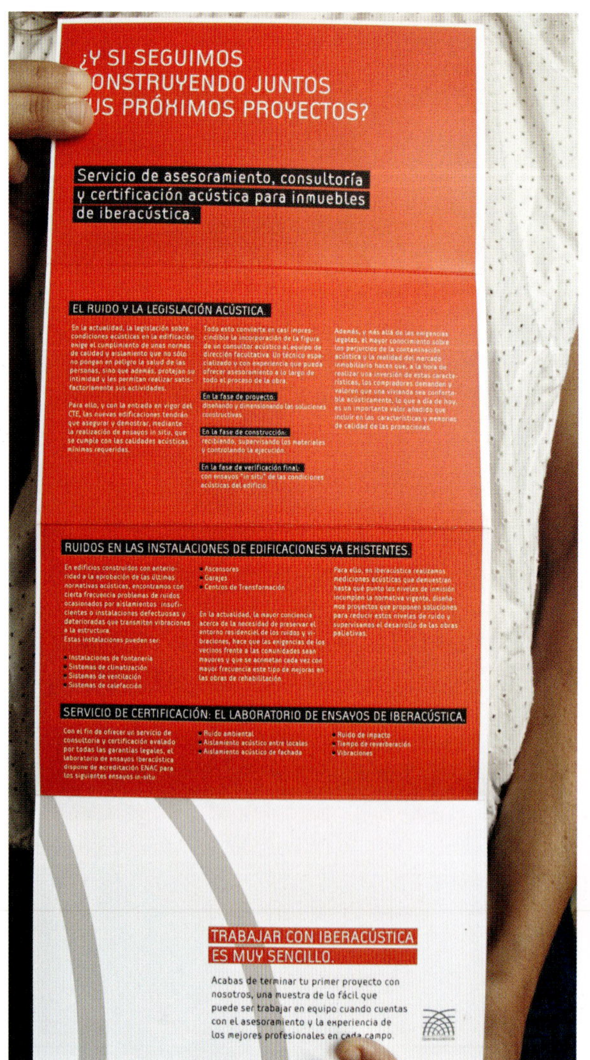

123/
picnic, ideas surtidas • *Informational brochure for Iberacústica, a sound engineering company*

www.iberacustica.com
iberacústica

¿Y SI EMPEZAMOS
A CONSTRUIR JUNTOS?
Juan García
COL. ARQUITECTOS
c/Gerrena 6
07002 Palma

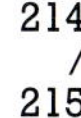

Menta • *Poster, when unfolded, highlighting the main design element, photography*

125/
dot. • *Pamphlet for Plan Renove electrical motors*

Andalucía A+
Plan renove
motores eléctricos
Ahórrate energía

Plan renove
motores eléctricos
Reducción d
las pé
de
ha
un
11,4%

Atelier Flora • *Catalogue promoting the artists, services, and clients of Atelier Flora*

CLIENTS
BOOKS
CONTACT

127/
Marisa Gallén • *Fold-out catalogue for the Ones exhibition*

128/
Rafael Maia • *Folder/poster announcing the dance spectacle from ballet dancer and choreographer Adriana Banana*

129/
Álvaro Sanchis • *Poster/informational pamphlet designed for the promotional campaign of the Master's Degree Program in Design and Illustration of the UPV*

E
DIN
META
HELVETICA
M
10/11
máster en
Diseño e Ilustración

M
10/11
máster en
Diseño e Ilustración

130/
POLIEDRO studio • *Brochure/poster promoting the restoration of a historic village church in Telgate*

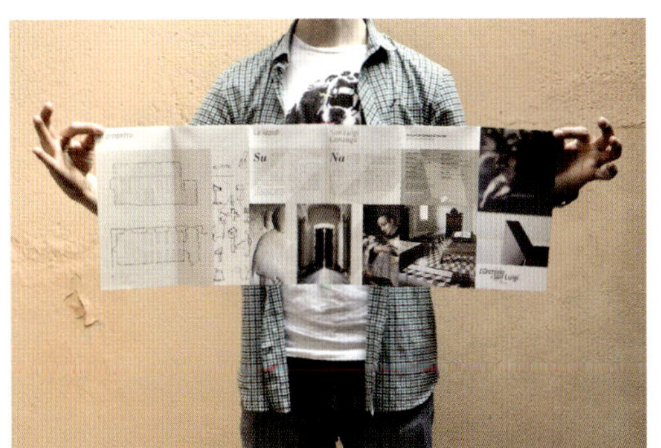

ENFÁTIKA • *Programme of music, spectacle, dance and theatre festivities of Santomera*

24.SEP
FESTIVAL DE DANZA
25.SEP
III FESTIVAL INTERNACIONAL DE DANZAS ÁRABES BELLYSAN
EL PUCHERO DEL HORTELANO
26.SEP
EFECTO MARIPOSA
27.SEP
28.SEP
HERMANOS MARX

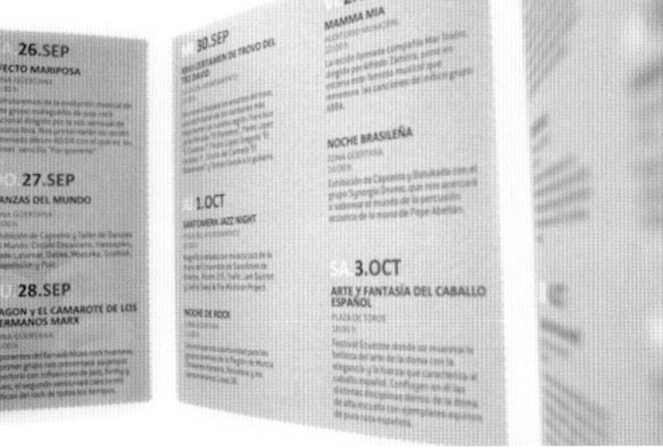
26.SEP
27.SEP
28.SEP
HERMANOS MARX
30.SEP
1.OCT
2.OCT
MAMMA MIA
NOCHE BRASILEÑA
3.OCT
ARTE Y FANTASÍA DEL CABALLO ESPAÑOL

132/
Atosio • *Brochure for the 2nd "Week of the Independent Publishing and Literature" (SELIN) held in Antequera*

EDITORIALES
Salto de Página/ Kalandraka/ Miguel Gómez Ediciones/ Nevsky Prospects/ Candaya/ Inéditor/ Alfama/ Alfar/ E.D.A. Libros/Aladena / El Olivo Azul/ Rey Lear / Del Planeta Rojo/ La Serranía/ Tropo/ Gens/ Escalera/Aljibe/ Traspiés/ GRUPO CONTEXTO: Libros del Asteroide, Barataria, Global Rhythm Press, Impedimenta, Nórdica, Periférica, Sexto Piso/ REPE: El Gaviero, Eclipsados, Huacanamo, Ya lo dijo Casimiro Parker, Cuatro de agosto, Labellavarsovia, Cangrejo Pistolero/
HORARIO Y UBICACIÓN FERIA DEL LIBRO
Ubicación Paseo Real.
ESPACIOS PARA ACTIVIDADES
SELIN
SEMANA DE LA EDICION Y LA LITERATURA INDEPENDIENTE
Antequera
Málaga
www.selin.es

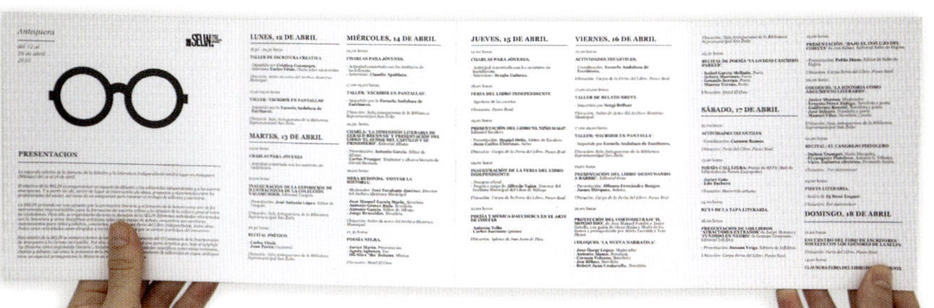
Antequera
PRESENTACION
LUNES, 12 DE ABRIL
MARTES, 13 DE ABRIL
MIÉRCOLES, 14 DE ABRIL
JUEVES, 15 DE ABRIL
VIERNES, 16 DE ABRIL
SÁBADO, 17 DE ABRIL
DOMINGO, 18 DE ABRIL

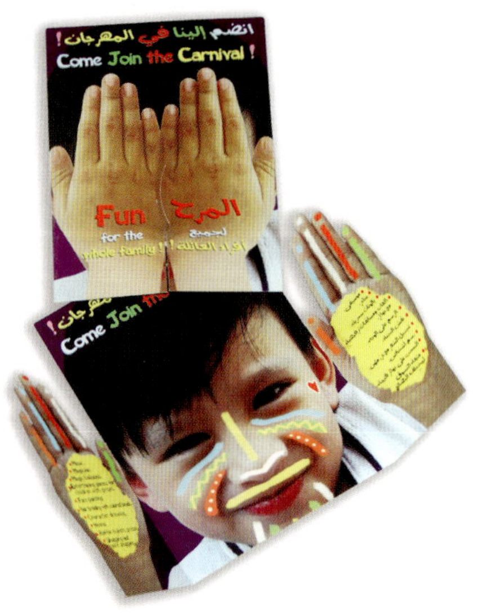

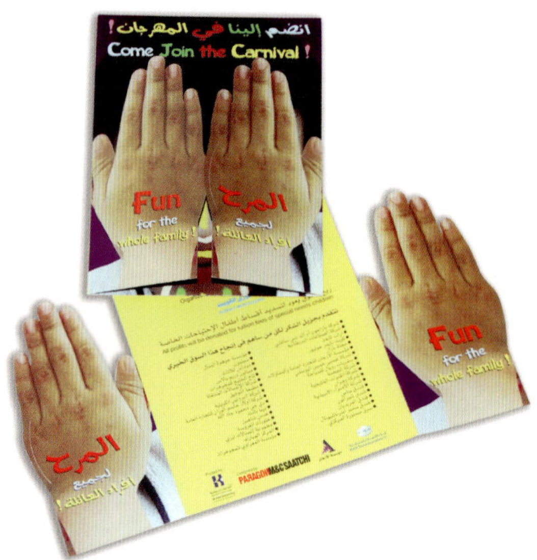

133/
Paragon Marketing Communications • *Brochure for a children's carnival by Kuwait Montessori*

extra! • *Program/poster Mercademostracions, Spain's most prestigious flower show*

135/
Dúctil • *Pamphlet promoting Menorca a la Vista, a photography conference*

MXM
MENORCA XARXA
MONUMENTAL
MENORCA A LA VISTA 2009
29, 30, 31 DE MAIG - 1 DE JUNY

MXM
MENORCA XARXA
MONUMENTAL
MENORCA A LA VISTA 2009
29, 30, 31 DE MAIG - 1 DE JUNY

Villuendas+Gómez Disseny • *Creation and design of brochure explaining the Cerdà Plan*

137/
Villuendas+Gómez Disseny • *Pamphlet promoting the exhibition Els feminismes de Feminal*

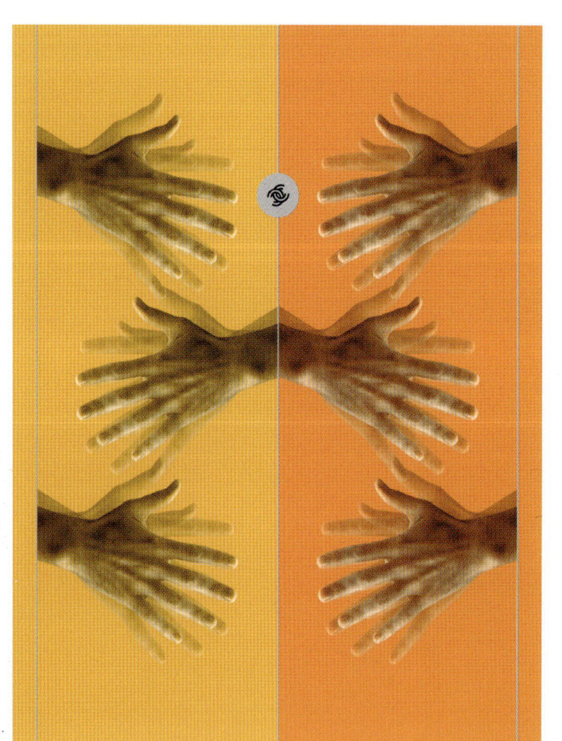

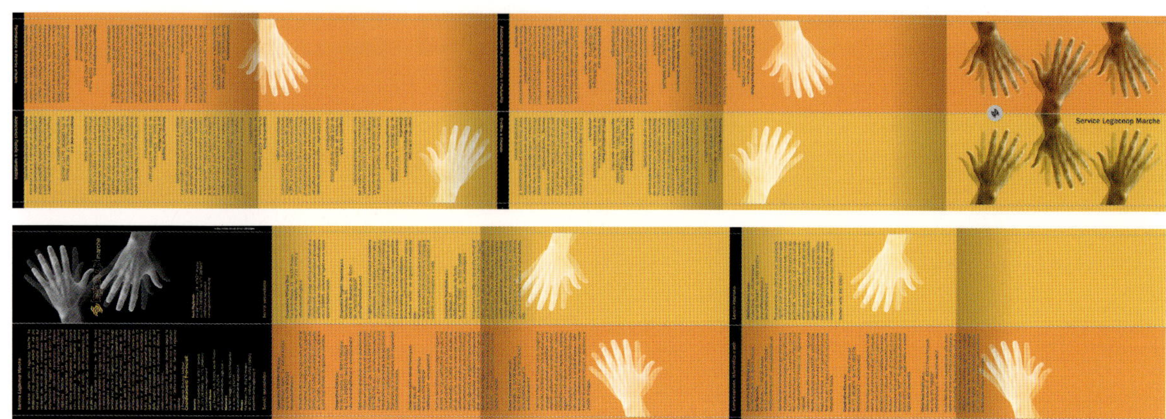

studiosancisi • *Brochures to promote the services*

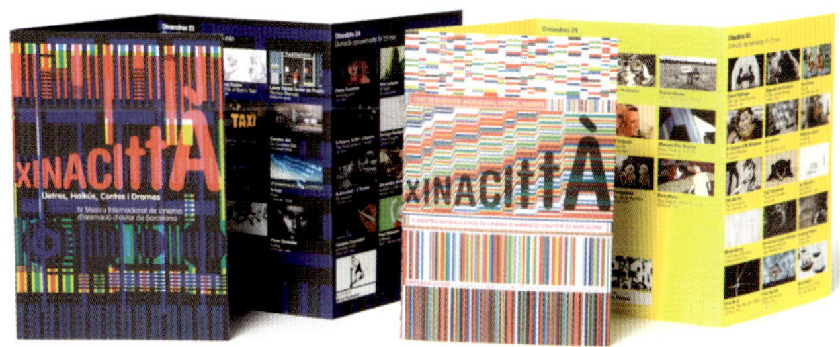

139/
David Torrents • *Programme promoting a festival of animation cinema*

Quattro idcp • *Specific mailing campaign that provides optical fiber network access to its recipients*

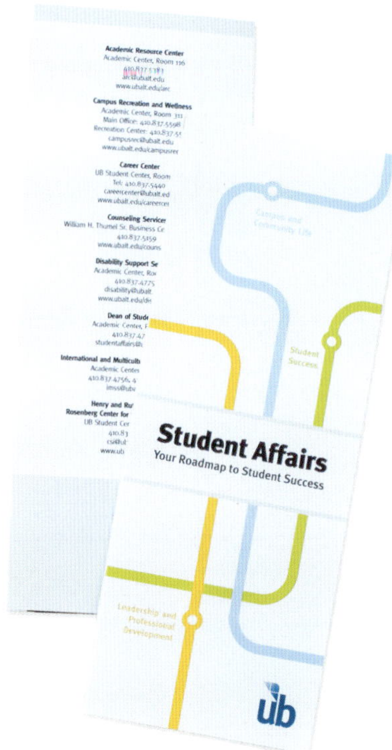

141/
University of Baltimore • *Brochure introducing students to the wide range of services and programs offered by the University of Baltimore Division of Enrollment Management and Student Affairs*

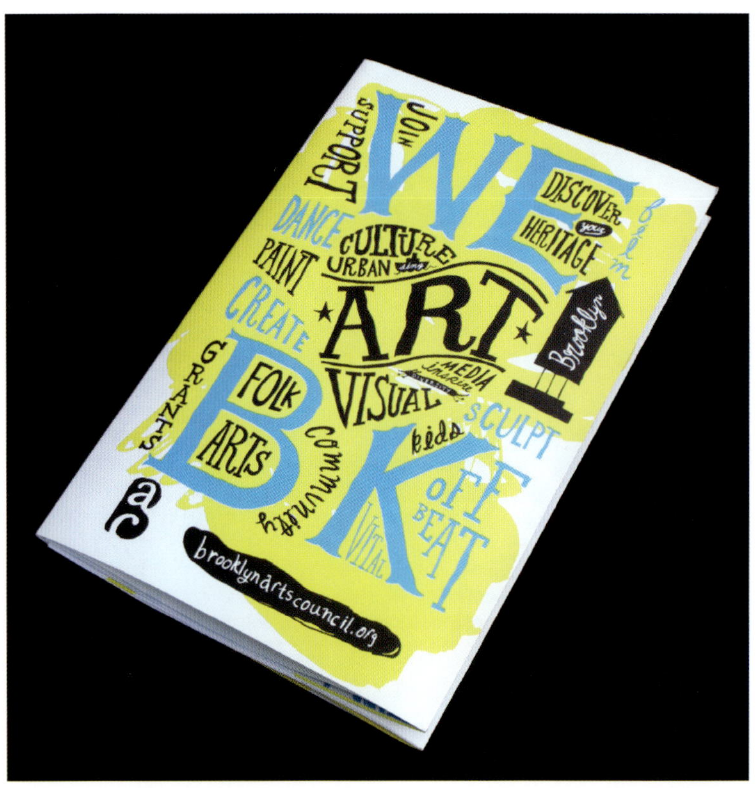

142/
Hyperakt • *Funky little identity piece that exudes the pride artists feel for Brooklyn and captures the energy of its art scene*

Multiple Folds

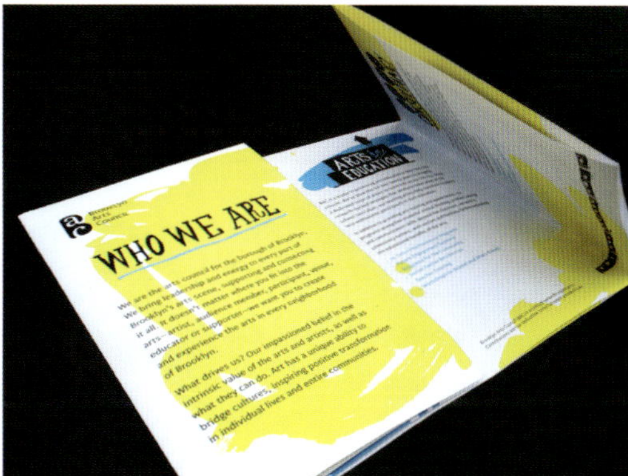

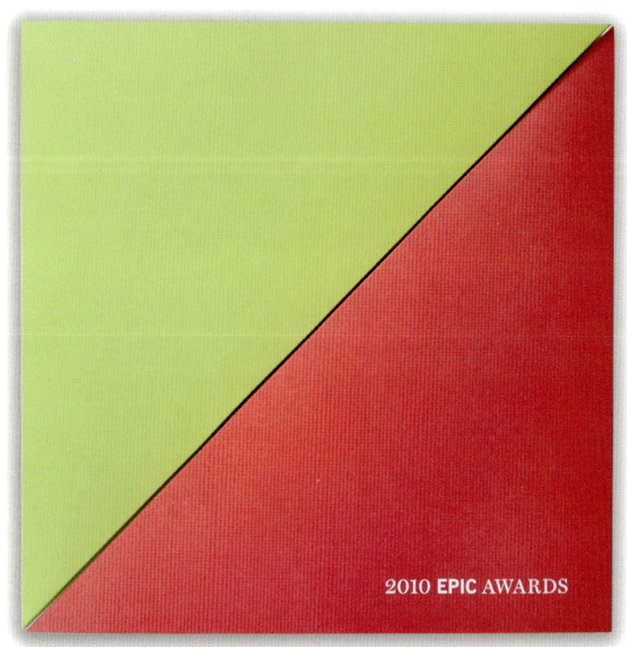

143/
Hyperakt • *Invitations to the The White House Project's 2010 EPIC Awards*

2010
EPIC
AWARDS

April 7, 2010
DINNER & AWARDS
6:00pm

Thonik • *Exhibition brochure for Atelier van Lieshout - Infernopolis*

er
lis

…ould be viewed not as
…s components of a group
… in which their (recent)

New partnership
Museum Boijmans Van Beuningen and the Port of Rotterdam have established a very special partnership. From 29 May until 26 September 2010 they are presenting *Infernopolis*, a thematic exhibition by the internationally renowned Atelier Van Lieshout, founded in 1995 by the Rotterdam-based artist Joep van Lieshout (1963). The exhibition takes place in the Submarine Wharf in Rotterdam's docklands. This gigantic building, with a surface area of almost 5000m², was constructed between 1929 and 1938. The wharf was used for building submarines and later become a storage space.

INFERNOPOLIS

The Technocrat

A good example is *The Technocrat*, an art work comprising apparatus, containers, beds and distillation kettles, grouped into four parts with obscure titles: *The Feeder, The Alcoholator, The Total Faecal Solution* and *The Participants*. Together they form a closed circuit of food, alcohol, excrement and energy. To function optimally *The Technocrat* requires a thousand people, or 'participants' as AVL calls them. They lie on bunk beds to save space and are stupefied by a permanent alcohol feed. Three times per day the participants are served a measured amount of specially prepared food, after which their bodies are sucked empty with the help of a vacuum pump.

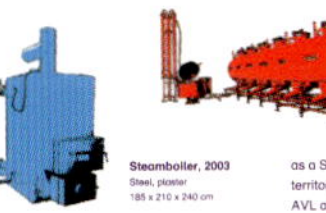
Alcoholator, 2004
Polyester
1050 x 220 x 260 cm

Steamboiler, 2003
Steel, plaster
185 x 210 x 240 cm

The yield then serves as the raw material for the following segment: *The Total Faecal Solution*, in which the faecal matter is heated and stirred. The gas produced by this process is then used to prepare a new batch of inexpensive food, with which the participants are fed, and so on.

The basis for *The Technocrat* was laid in an earlier art project: *AVL-Ville*. This anarchist Free State opened its doors in spring 2001 on a piece of derelict land directly adjoining AVL's workshop. '*AVL-Ville* is not an art work simply to be looked at, but is intended to be lived in', AVL announced in a press release at the time. The art work consisted of a community with its own flag, constitution and bank notes. *AVL-Ville* provided space to make art, free from laws and rules, and to live a self-sufficient and autonomous life. The residents operated their own hospital, farm, abattoir, restaurant, transport service and academy.

AVL-Ville was opposed t… forms of communal living… a utopia. Rather, AVL des… heterotopia: a space that… more, easier to realise. In… 'normal' society, *AVL-Vill*… Or to put it in other terms:… was parasitic on the existi… *AVL-Ville* offered an alter… which AVL believed to be… project's core was the qu… and rules enforced by the…

…as a State with its own lav… territory. To these symbol… AVL adds economic self-… cing its own food, energy,… arsenal, sanitation and w… tion, housing and medical… range of services that are… provided by the State.'

…o all other known… but was certainly not …cribed the village as a… is 'other' and, further-… stead of abolishing… e nestled within society. …the new AVL society …ng system. In essence, …native to our society, …overregulated. At the …ation: do the laws …State really serve our …collective interests? …AVL broached this …question by exposing …the government's …monopolistic position. …In an exhibition cata-…logue in 2001 the art …critic Jennifer Allen …concluded: 'AVL's …constitution, currency …and flag demonstrate …its political autonomy …vs, economy and …s of self-government, …sufficiency by produ-…drugs, alcohol, …ater systems, educa-…facilities – the whole …usually regulated or

Vacuum Tank, 2003
Polyester, steel
150 x 150 x 275 cm

The freedom that AVL aspired to could be achieved only when there was self-sufficiency on all fronts. This approach implied a constant search for inventive solutions and a free spirit.

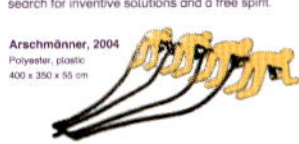
Arschmänner, 2004
Polyester, plastic
400 x 350 x 55 cm

To meet these demands, AVL employed what it called 'Solvism', an ideology aimed at 'finding solutions and solving problems'. This philosophy was used to tackle the problem of how to process *AVL-Ville*'s waste, the answer to which turned out to be recycling. Given that faeces can be recycled with the help of biogas, Joep van Lieshout designed a biogas installation for *AVL-Ville*.

Watertower, 2003
Polyester, steel
200 x 200 x 800 cm

Autocomposter, 2003
Polyester, steel
180 x 180 x 560 cm

When, after seven months, the local council forced AVL to close the commune, the so-called *Biodigester* was still in development. Following the closure of *AVL-Ville*, Atelier Van Lieshout continued to investigate systems and models, and the *Biodigester* was developed further and realised as a component of *The Technocrat*, which is now displayed in the Submarine Wharf.

INFERNOPOLIS

Systems and organs

Central to *The Technocrat* is a ruthless form of recycling in which humans are reduced to mechanical components: cogs in the machine. To emphasise this aspect, the participants are designed to be completely identical and interchangeable, like nuts and bolts in a larger system. Non-functioning participants are replaced immediately. As in many of AVL's projects the distinction between man and machine has been erased.

AVL also views the human body as a machine full of moving parts. For example, the massive organ sculptures such as the polyester penises in small, medium, large and extra large versions (2003) and the 16-metre-long sculpture *BarRectum* (2005) represent individual body parts but also interconnected, internal systems.

BarRectum, 2005
Polyester
800 x 800 x 250 cm

Penis S, M, XL, 2003
Polyester
175 x 85 x 90 cm
206 x 80 x 123 cm
350 x 175 x 205 cm

Joep van Lieshout: 'I like to work with organs in order to show something of the beauty of our insides and the system behind it. Why does it look like this, why is it made like this? These are almost existential questions.'

The sculptures placed throughout the Submarine Wharf reveal the hidden system of glands, blood vessels, muscle groups and organs.

Although the organ sculptures are anatomically correct and give us an insight into how the human body is designed, their meaning is to be found, above all, in the similarities between large, coordinated models (society) and intimate, personal systems (the body and its organs). For example, the digestive system bears comparison with the world at large, which also consumes

…and produces. Both of th… in the architectural work… work, which represents t… digestive system (from t… drink a beer in the reddis…

Reproduction

Life and death are equall… AVL's *Infernopolis*. The r… coloured polyester recrea…

Wombhouse, 2004
Polyester
630 x 236 x 212 cm

…female reproductive orga… symbols. A good example… architectural work *Womb*… of an immense, polyester… component of the work h… of the ovaries houses a t… functions as a minibar wit… of spirits and a champagn… most important compone… cavity, furnished with a large comfortable bed. Visitors may lie on the bed, suggesting a similarity with new life or the unborn child.

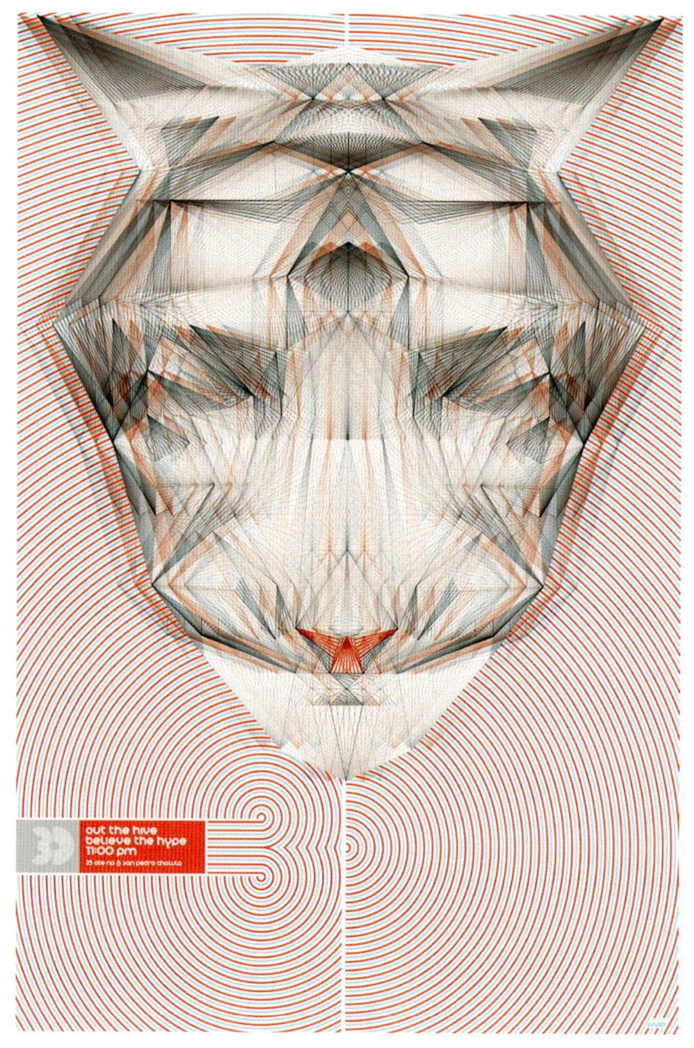

145/
poeticsouvenir • *3D + Out the hive believe the hype. Invitation for a private Le Tigre DJ set party, produced by Will produce for food*

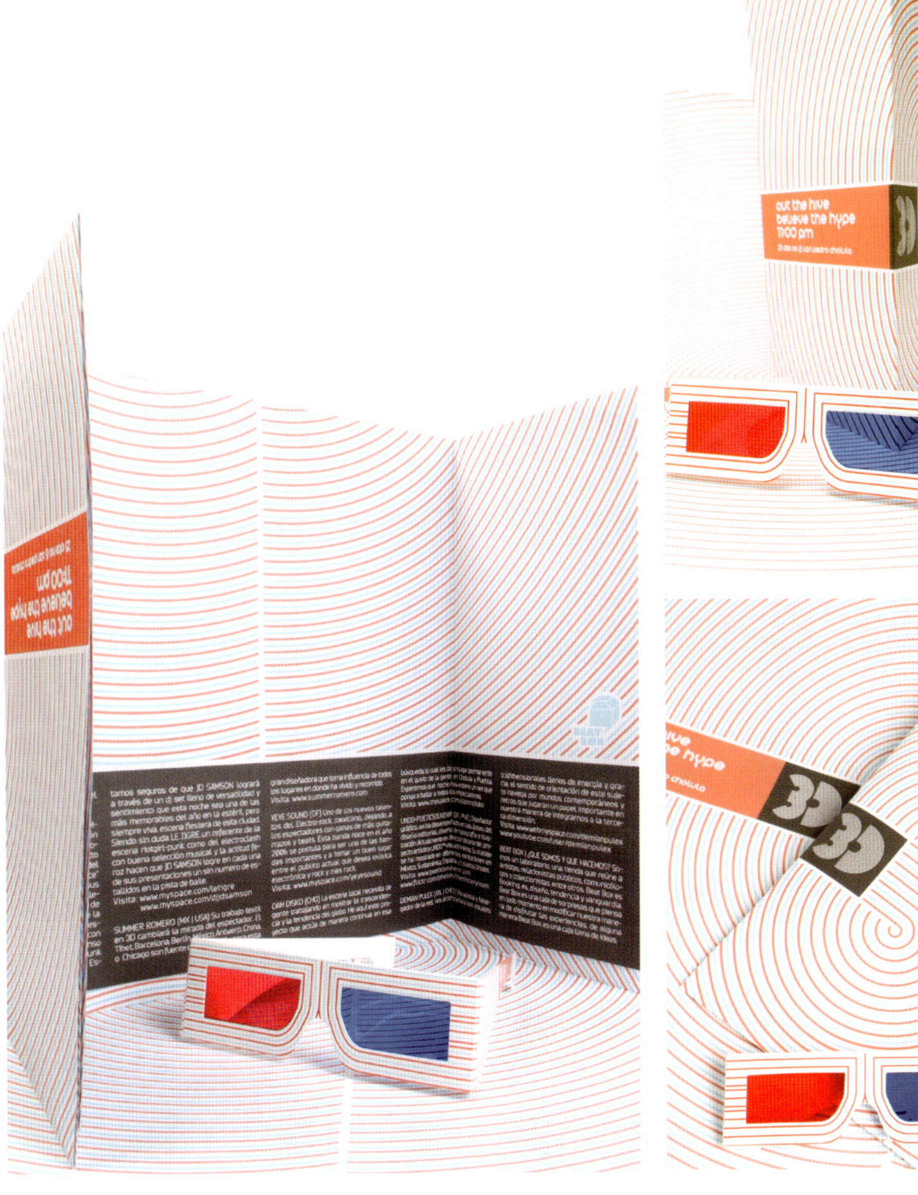
out the hive
believe the hype
11:00 pm
BEAT BOX

Nifava • *Informational brochure promoting the 9th Festival of Jazz of Girona*

Festival de Jazzcw`eolvw fjawldkvas+kad ñlvçalsv`cs de Girona
Presentació

Festival de Jazzcw`eolvw fjawldkvas+kad ñlvçalsv`cs de Girona

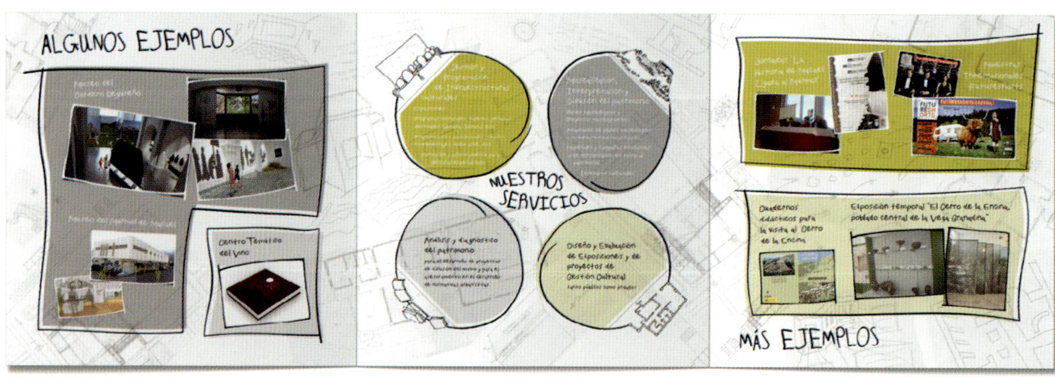

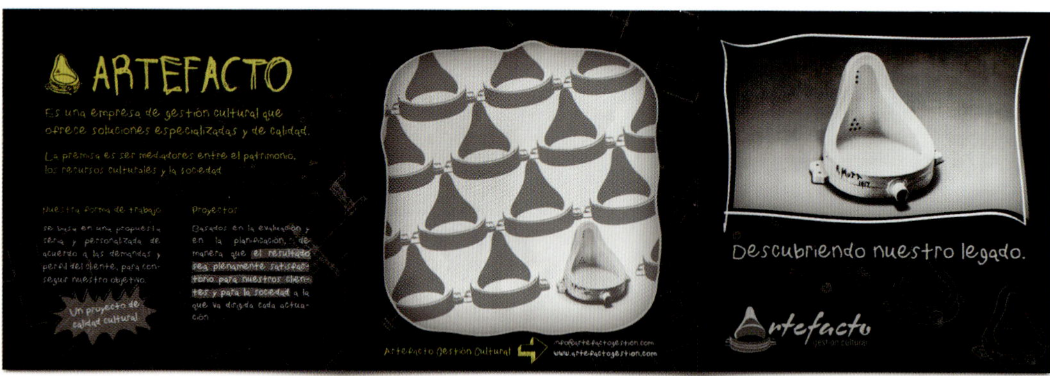

Ártico Estudio • *Folder/catalogue explaining Artefacto, its available services, clients, and selected works*

ALGUNOS EJEMPLOS
ARTEFACTO
NUESTROS SERVICIOS
MÁS EJEMPLOS
Descubriendo nuestro legado.

NUESTROS SERVICIOS
Análisis y diagnóstico del patrimonio
Diseño y Evaluación de Exposiciones y de proyectos de Gestión Cultural
Centro Temático del Vino
Cuadernos didácticos para la visita al Cerro de la Encina

148/
dot. • *Fold-out pamphlet explaining all the publications and projects of this publishing house*

149/
Dúctil • *Pamphlet explaining the commitment of Editorial Rotger towards the creativity and the design*

150/
Xavier Lanau • *Flyer and poster for the Killda 10th anniversary party. Barcelona-based dj's collective*

BLOWING
UP BALLOON
presents.
KILLDA
10 YEARS
Dissabte
31 Octubre
2009

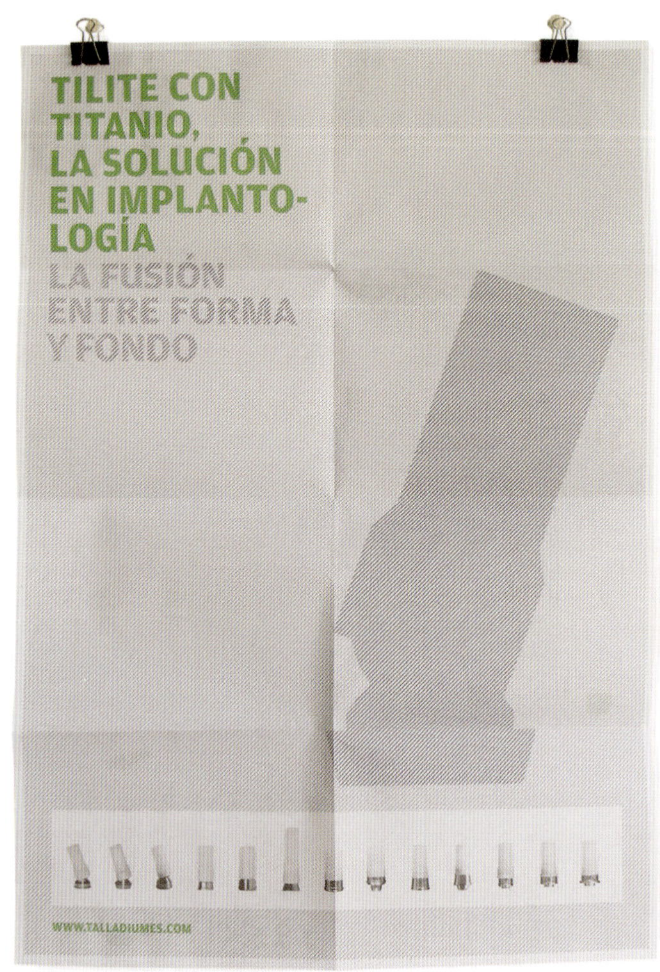

151/
Oxigen comunicació gràfica • *Product pamphlet for a designer and manufacturer specialising in dental prostheses*

LOGÍA

LA FUSIÓN
ENTRE FORMA
Y FONDO
TALLADIUM
TALLADIUM SPAIN

LA COMBI-
NACIÓN
PERFECTA
TALLADIUM ESPAÑA HA CONSEGUIDO UNIR EL FONDO Y LA FORMA. LA COMBINACIÓN PERFECTA, PARA FACILITAR SOLU- CIONES EFICACES A LOS PROFESIONALES DEL SECTOR. UNA FUSIÓN QUE SE REFLEJA EN SU AMPLIA GAMA DE PRODUCTOS Y SERVICIOS.
filosofía es avanzar, investigar y ofrecer soluciones. Ser la pieza clave del sector.
LA PIEZA CLAVE
CATÁLOGO DESPLEGABLE

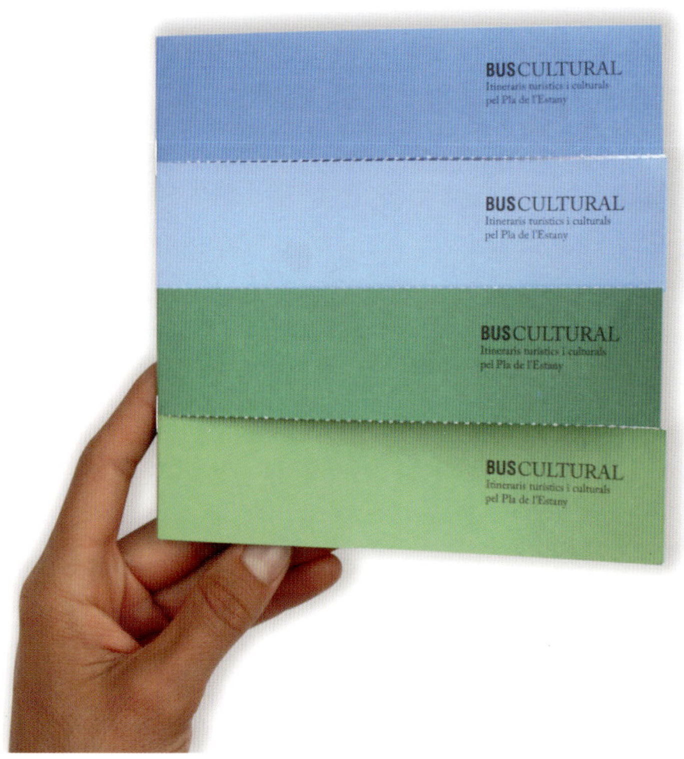

Nifava • *Pamphlet explaining how Bus Cultural helps visitors learn the cultural heritage of del Pla de l'Estany*

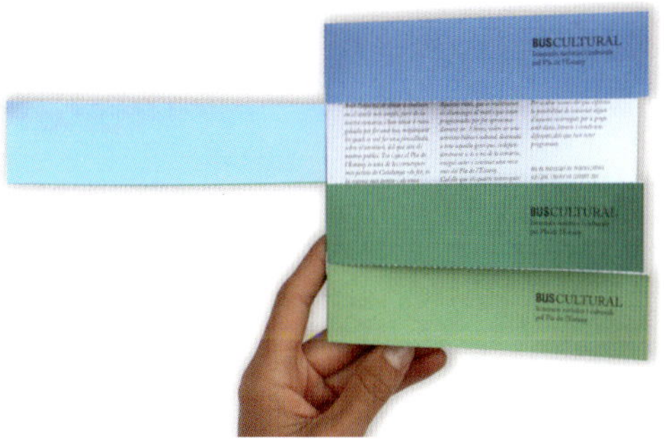
BUSCULTURAL
BUSCULTURAL
BUSCULTURAL

BUSCULTURAL
BUSCULTURAL

RUTA 1
RUTA 2
BANYOLES, VILADEMULS
I CORNELLÀ DEL TERRI
RUTA 3
FONTCOBERTA, ESPONELLÀ
I CRESPIÀ
RUTA 4
CAMÓS, PALOL DE REVARDIT
I CORNELLÀ DEL TERRI

153/
Pau Lamuà • *Single fold catalogue designed for the exhibition 1M2, the cover of the catalogue is a folded poster*

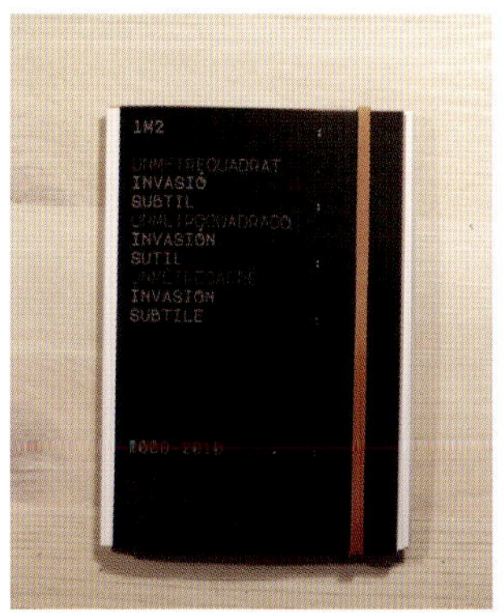
1M2
INVASIÓ
SUBTIL
INVASIÓN
SUTIL
INVASION
SUBTILE

1M2
UNMETREQUADRAT
INVASIÓ
SUBTIL
INVASIÓN
SUTIL
INVASION
SUBTILE

CAT
NOUS
ITINERARIS
PER LA CULTURA

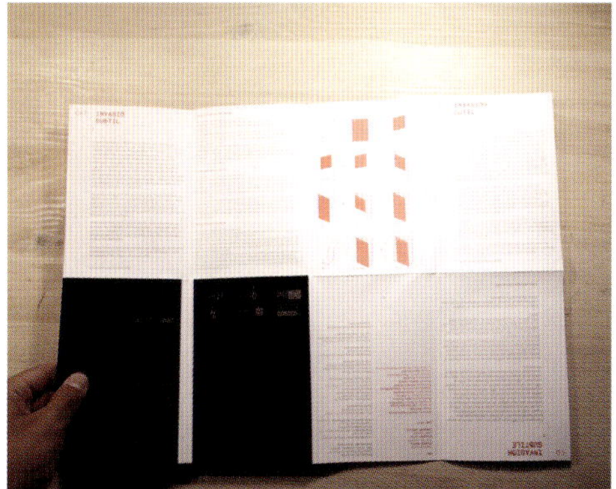

1M2
INVASIÓ
SUBTIL
INVASIÓN

154/
Root Studio • *Brochure promoting Lincs Design Consultancy, a UK firm offering architectural, planning and environmental consulting*

155/
El vivero • *Fold-out programme featuring children's film*

VIS-TEK • *Product folder and cards for Aquagest Solutions*

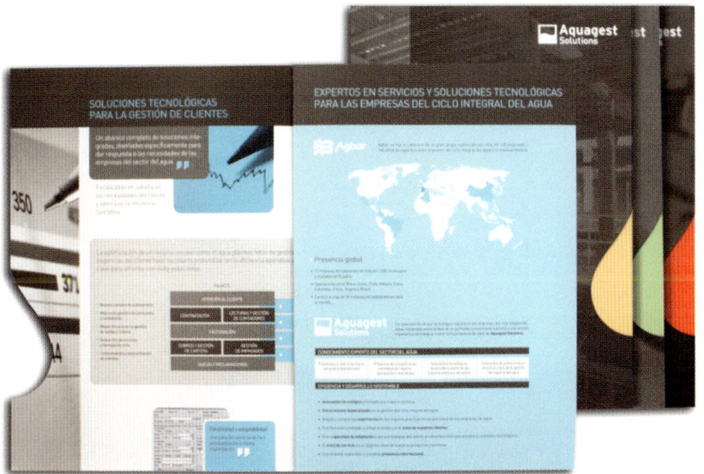
Aquagest Solutions
SOLUCIONES TECNOLÓGICAS
PARA LA GESTIÓN DE CLIENTES
EXPERTOS EN SERVICIOS Y SOLUCIONES TECNOLÓGICAS
PARA LAS EMPRESAS DEL CICLO INTEGRAL DEL AGUA
Agbar
Presencia global
Aquagest Solutions

Aquagest Solutions
TI
TECNOLOGÍAS
DE LA INFORMACIÓN
SOLUCIONES, CONSULTORÍA
Y OUTSOURCING DE PROCESOS

157/
VIS-TEK • *Folder with catalogue highlighting Nuevo Polo, a new car model from Volkswagen*

158/
Base Design • *Brochure for the new Plus Series line from Pantone®*

159/
Base Design • *Capital campaign brochure for the Miami Art Museum*

THE NEW FACE OF M!AM!

MAKING GREATER MIAMI GREATER

Miami is an international creative capital, a city whose greatest resource is its people. The new Miami Art Museum will capture the city's distinctive multicultural dynamism and serve as a resource for all of Miami. The new Miami Art Museum will be welcoming and exciting, an institution that will provide our community with great art and enriching education programs for generations to come.

MAM has entered into a public/private partnership with the City of Miami and Miami-Dade County to build a new civic resource for the city. A dramatic location on Biscayne Bay has been provided by the city of Miami, and the voters of Miami-Dade County have already approved $100 million in funding. The new Miami Art Museum, together with the new Miami Science Museum, will revitalize downtown, and transform Museum Park into a vibrant destination on Miami's cultural map.

INSPIRING!

Designed by celebrated architects Herzog & de Meuron, the new Miami Art Museum building will seamlessly weave together the museum and the park. Herzog & de Meuron have conceived an innovative, state-of-the-art facility for MAM that will advance the goals of the institution and support the continued growth of its collection.

Recipients of some of architecture's most prestigious awards, including the Pritzker Prize, the Royal Gold Medal for Architecture and the Praemium Imperiale, Herzog & de Meuron are known for designs that are inventive, and sensitive to the site and culture of their surroundings. Their work includes such critically acclaimed projects as the Walker Arts Center in Minneapolis, the de Young Museum in San Francisco and the Tate Modern in London.

GROWING!

The new, 125,000-square-foot MAM will more than double its current exhibition space and attract more than four times its current number of visitors. Already home to the largest art museum education program in Miami-Dade County, MAM's new building will include an education center devoted to significantly increasing its educational programming and outreach. New classrooms, meeting spaces, an auditorium and expanded resources will provide greater opportunities for children, students, adults, special needs audiences and seniors to actively learn about and experience the life-enhancing power of art.

MAM's new building will provide 32,000 square feet of gallery space—enough to display the current collection and foster its ongoing growth. With the announcement of MAM's new building, the Museum's collection has increased dramatically, with gifts of more than 150 works of art within a 12-month period. Additionally, this expanded, centrally located space was a major factor leading to MAC-MAM, the groundbreaking collaboration with Miami Art Central.

Amenities such as a cafe, museum store and ample parking in the building's lower levels will further serve MAM's visitors. The museum's shaded outdoor terrace and surrounding sculptures will be accessible to all, not just those who enter the museum. Thus, the new MAM will educate and inspire everyone, nurturing the creative energy that makes Miami a great place to live, work and visit.

isebuki / collabor.at • *Concept design of a brochure/map of local artists*

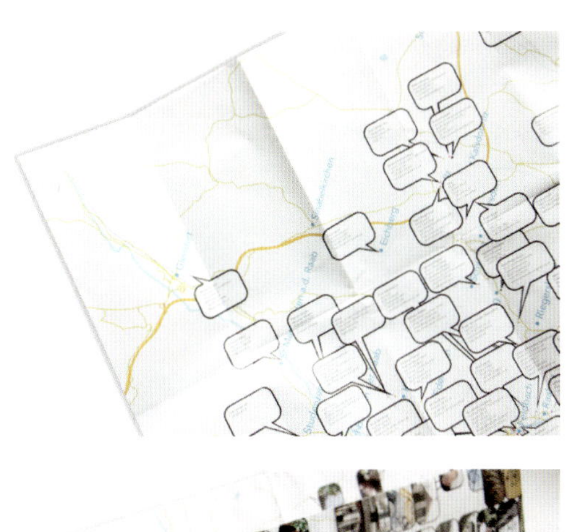

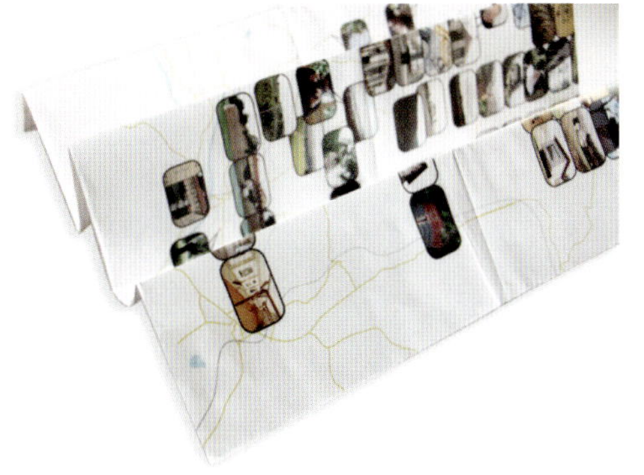

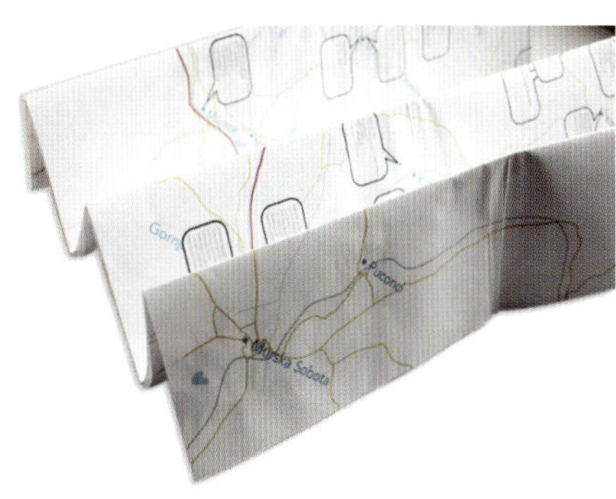
Puconci
Murska Sobota

161/
studiosancisi • *Brochure promoting the restaurant Kentaro*

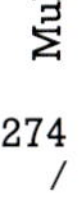

162/
studiosancisi • *Brochure explaining rasterpunch, a new technology product*

163/
Bunch • *Colorful brochure for Hortiart, a gardening studio*

hortiart

PAPARAJOTE • *Folder made of recycled cardboard and containing individual cards that group six thematic bicycle itineraries to discover La Huerta de Murcia autumn*

VIVIENDO
LA HUERTA
EN BICI

¡Ven a disfrutar de la huerta pedaleando y descubre un mundo muy nuestro, muy próximo y muy desconocido!
VIVIENDO
LA HUERTA
EN BICI

¡Ven a disfrutar de la huerta pedaleando y descubre un mundo muy nuestro, muy próximo y muy desconocido!
1.
RUTA DE AUROROS Y TRADICIONES
21sep08
1. RUTA DE AUROROS Y TRADICIONES 21sep08
2. RUTA DEL AGUA 28sep08
3. RUTA DE LAS ERMITAS 05oct08
4. RUTA BOTÁNICA 12oct08
5. RUTA DE LAS CASAS TORRE 19oct08
6. RUTA DE LOS CASTILLOS 26oct08

projectGRAPHICS • *Brochure for the play The Last Supper*

166/
PAPARAJOTE • *Brochure promoting the bicycle transport*

167/
brand attack • *Brochure promoting the product line Bargalló oil for commercial sale*

100 MAGNUM
100 MAGNUM
100 MAGNUM
100 MAGNUM
Olis Bargalló

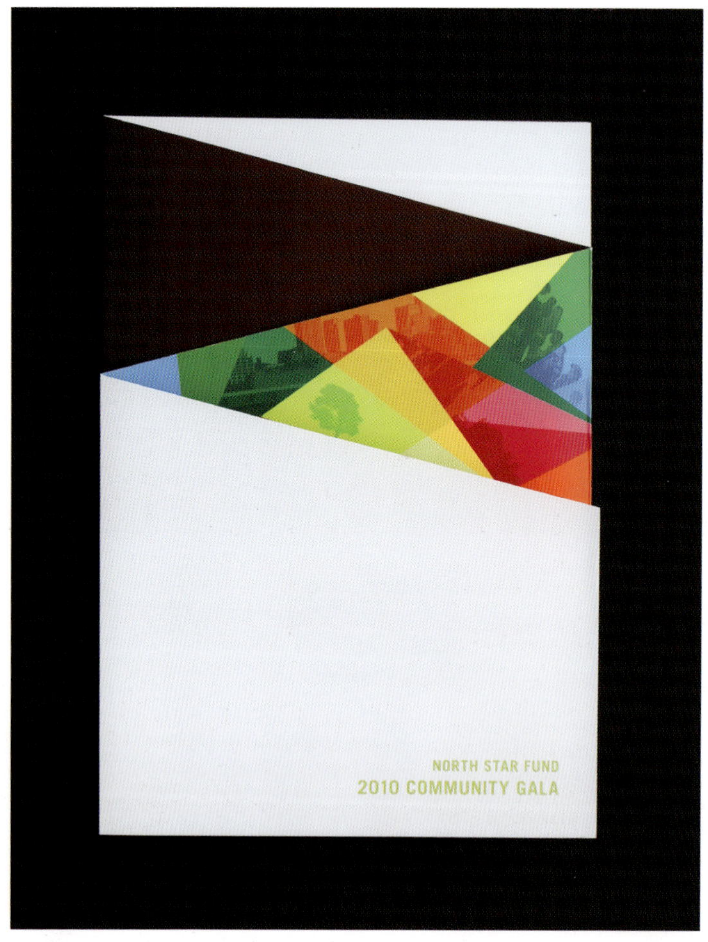

Hyperakt • *Invitations and the event programme for North Star Fund 2010 Community Gala*

NORTH STAR FUND
2010 COMMUNITY GALA
THURSDAY, APRIL 29, 2010

169/
Base Design • *Brochure for the San Francisco Art Institute as part of its identity design*

seeing
BOMB
engaging
innovating
sfai

170/
Quattro idcp • *Pamphlet communicating advantages of the corporate use of cable-less Internet*

171/
THIS IS Studio • *Show catalogue for the students of the Masters of Fine Art Goldsmiths*

Buenaidea/ José Fernández Oyarzábal • *Double pamphlet The Roman Theatre of Malaga and The launching Slips of History*

173/
Jessie Whipple Vickery • *Series of brochures highlighting the different processes found within the coffee industry*

PAPARAJOTE • *Catalogue for Titis Summer 2010.*

175/
studiosancisi • *Brochures promoting the services of IN.D.A.CO.*

001/ - Brochure number
lila&tom / Anna Farré - Studio name
La Compagnie des Petits - Client name
Spain - Country

Children's Fashion Collection 2010-2011
for La Compagnie des Petits - Brochure description

105/
ATIPUS
ATIPUS
Spain

Promotional catalogue detailing 10 years of strategic design from Atipus, including selected examples of the studio's work

106/
Erretres Diseño
SEEI
Spain

Exhibition pamphlet

107/
Nifava
Projecte Sonora i El Foment de Banyoles
Spain

Image of S de Saderra show, designed specifically as a tribute to the Catalan composer of sardanas Manel Saderra

108/
Oxigen comunicació gràfica
yellow ideas
Spain

Fold-out pamphlet that details the different lectures and creativity seminars offered by Yellow Ideas

109/
ENFÁTIKA
Grupo Hefame
Spain

Internal marketing campaign to encourage employees to submit ideas on how their company and workplace can be improved

110/
Diseño Cdroig
Fernando Gil
Spain

Prestigious graphic design pamphlet

111/
Erretres Diseño
ICEX
Spain

Pamphlet designed for FHA2010, an international food and hospitality trade exposition held in Singapore

112/
Ideario Chinín
Ayuntamiento de Soneja
Spain

Pamphlet highlighting the programme of commemorative acts in recognition of the 400th anniversary of the charter of the town Soneja

113/
Blok Design
El Zanjon
Mexico

Visitors' guide brochure for El Zanjón, historic building in Buenos Aires

114/
Cubo Diseño
DINÓPOLIS
Spain

Press dossier for Dinópolis, a dinosaur theme park, which was distributed during the international exposition of Zaragoza

115/
CADG
theCHgallery
Spain

Pamphlet for photography studio

116/
oikos associati
OmniDecor®
Italy

Fold-out brochure for DecorTile, a product line from OmniDecor®

117/
Nifava
Consorci de Benestar Social del Pla de l'Estany-Banyoles
Spain

Accordion-fold brochure promoting a film series on issues related to social inclusion

118/
ENFÁTIKA
Concejalía de Cultura. Ayuntamiento de Santomera, Murcia
Spain

Programme of the Certamen Contest

119/
Sublima Comunicación
CENDEAC
Spain

Pamphlet for the new course from Centro de Documentación y Estudios Avanzados de Arte Contemporáneo (CENDEAC)

120/
Thonik
Spiral
Netherlands

Design of the corporate identity and campaign to mark the 25th anniversary of the Tokyo art institution, Spiral

121/
Miller Meiers Design for Communication
One Point Security Solutions
United States (USA)

Introductory brochure explaining the services of One Point Security Solutions

122/
dot.
Andalucía Emprende, Fundación Pública Andaluza
Spain

Pamphlet daily programmes of an entrepreneur in Andalusia.

123/
picnic, ideas surtidas
iberacústica
Spain

Informational brochure for Iberacústica, a sound engineering company

124/
Menta
Tomás Llavador Arquitectos+Ingenieros
Spain

Poster, when unfolded, highlighting the main design element, photography

125/
dot.
Agencia Andaluza de la Energía
Spain

Pamphlet for Plan Renove electrical motors

126/
Atelier Flora
Atelier Flora
Germany

Catalogue promoting the artists, services, and clients of Atelier Flora

127/
Marisa Gallén
Federación Empresarial de Hostelerìa de Valencia
Spain

Fold-out catalogue for the Ones exhibition

128/
Rafael-Maia
Adriana Banana
Brasil

Folder/poster announcing the dance spectacle from ballet dancer and choreographer Adriana Banana

129/
Álvaro Sanchis
Universidad Politécnica de Valencia
Spain

Poster/informational pamphlet designed for the promotional campaign of the Master's Degree Program in Design and Illustration of the UPV.

130/
POLIEDRO studio
Parrocchia di Telgate (Bg)
Italy

Brochure/poster promoting the restoration of a historic village church in Telgate

131/
ENFÁTIKA
Concejalía de Cultura. Ayuntamiento de Santomera , Murcia
Spain

Programme of music, spectacle, dance and theatre festivities of Santomera

132/
Atosio
SELIN:SEMANA DE LA EDICIÓN Y LA LITERATURA INDEPENDIENTE
Spain

Brochure for the 2nd "Week of the Independent Publishing and Literature" (SELIN) held in Antequera

133/
Paragon Marketing Communications
Kuwait Montessori
Kuwait

Brochure for a children's carnival by Kuwait Montessori

134/
extra!
Mercabarna
Spain

Program/poster Mercademostracions, Spain's most prestigious flower show

135/
Dúctil
Foto Club Llum. Ferreries
Spain

Pamphlet promoting Menorca a la Vista, a photography conference

136/
Villuendas+Gómez Disseny
Turismo de Barcelona
Spain

Creation and design of brochure explaining the Cerdà Plan

137/
Villuendas+Gómez Disseny
Institut Català de les Dones. Generalitat de Catalunya
Spain

Pamphlet promoting the exhibition Els feminismes de Feminal

138/
studiosancisi
Legacoop Marche
Italy

Brochures to promote the services

139/
David Torrents
APQR
Spain

Programme promoting a festival of animation cinema

140/
Quattro idcp
R, cable y telecomunicaciones
Spain

Specific mailing campaign that provides optical fiber network access to its recipients

141/
University of Baltimore
Division of Enrollment Management and Student Affairs
United States (USA)

Brochure introducing students to the wide range of services and programs offered by the University of Baltimore Division of Enrollment Management and Student Affairs

142/
Hyperakt
The Brooklyn Arts Council
United States

Funky little identity piece that exudes the pride artists feel for Brooklyn and captures the energy of its art scene

143/
Hyperakt
The White House Project
United States

Invitations to the The White House Project's 2010 EPIC Awards

144/
Thonik
Museum Boijmans van Beuningen
Netherlands

Exhibition brochure for Atelier van Lieshout - Infernopolis

145/
poeticsouvenir
Will produce for food
México

3D + Out the hive believe the hype. Invitation for a private Le Tigre DJ set party, produced by Will produce for food

146/
Nifava
Ajuntament de Girona Muass, Músics Associats
Spain

Informational brochure promoting the 9th Festival of Jazz of Girona.

147/
Ártico Estudio
Artefacto Gestión Cultural
Spain

Folder/catalogue explaining Artefacto, its available services, clients, and selected works

148/
dot.
La Máquina China
Spain

Fold-out pamphlet explaining all the publications and projects of this publishing house.

149/
Dúctil
Editorial Rotger
Spain

Pamphlet explaining the commitment of Editorial Rotger towards the creativity and the design

150/
Xavier Lanau
Killda
Spain

Flyer and poster for the Killda 10th anniversary party. Barcelona-based dj's collective

151/
Oxigen comunicació gràfica
Talladium
Spain

Product pamphlet for a designer and manufacturer specialising in dental prostheses

152/
Nifava
Consell Comarcal del Pla de l'Estany
Spain

Pamphlet explaining how Bus Cultural helps visitors learn the cultural heritage of del Pla de l'Estany

153/
Pau Lamuà
Institut de Cultura de la Ciutat d'Olot
Spain

Single fold catalogue designed for the exhibition 1M2, the cover of the catalogue is a folded poster

154/
Root Studio
Lincs Design Consultancy
United Kingdom

Brochure promoting Lincs Design Consultancy, a UK firm offering architectural, planning and environmental consulting

155/
El vivero
Museo Nacional Centro de Arte Reina Sofía, Madrid
Spain

Fold-out programme featuring children's film

156/
VIS-TEK
Agbar Agua
Spain

Product folder and cards for Aquagest Solutions

157/
VIS-TEK
Volkwagen España
Spain

Folder with catalogue highlighting Nuevo Polo, a new car model from Volkswagen

158/
Base Design
Pantone
United States (USA)

Brochure for the new Plus Series line from Pantone®

159/
Base Design
Miami Art Museum
United States (USA)

Capital campaign brochure for the Miami Art Museum

160/
isebuki / collabor.at
regionale08 – festival for contemporary art
Austria

Concept design of a brochure/map of local artists

161/
studiosancisi
kentaro
Italy

Brochure promoting the restaurant Kentaro

162/
studiosancisi
Grossi lamiere
Italy

Brochure explaining rasterpunch, a new technology product

163/
Bunch
Hortiart
United Kingdom

Colorful brochure for Hortiart, a gardening studio

164/
PAPARAJOTE
Asociación Murcia en bici
Spain

Folder made of recycled cardboard and containing individual cards that group six thematic bicycle itineraries to discover La Huerta de Murcia autumn

165/
projectGRAPHICS
Multimedia Center
Kosovo

Brochure for the play The Last Supper

166/
PAPARAJOTE
CONBICI
Coordinadora en Defensa de la Bici
Spain

Brochure promoting the bicycle transport

167/
brand attack
Olis Bargalló
Spain

Brochure promoting the product line Bargalló oil for commercial sale

168/
Hyperakt
North Star Fund
United States

Invitations and the event programme for North Star Fund 2010 Community Gala

169/
Base Design
San Francisco Art Institute
United States (USA)

Brochure for the San Francisco Art Institute as part of its identity design

170/
Quattro idcp
R, cable y telecomunicaciones
Spain

Pamphlet communicating advantages of the corporate use of cable-less Internet

171/
THIS IS Studio
Communications and Publicity Goldsmiths
United Kingdom

Show catalogue for the students of the Masters of Fine Art Goldsmiths

172/
Buenaidea - José Fernández Oyarzábal
Teatro Romano de Málaga. Consejería de Cultura de la Junta de Andalucía
Spain

Double pamphlet The Roman Theatre of Malaga and The launching Slips of History

173/
Jessie Whipple Vickery
Stumptown Coffee Roasters
United States (USA)

Series of brochures highlighting the different processes found within the coffee industry

174/
PAPARAJOTE
Titis Clothing
Spain

Catalogue for Titis Summer 2010.

175/
studiosancisi
Indaco
Italy

Brochures promoting the services of IN.D.A.CO.

Final Directory
300 - 305

2FRESH - studio name
053/ - brochure number
http://www.2fresh.com/ - studio website

2FRESH
053/
http://www.2fresh.com/

Alambre Estudio
064/ 073/
www.alambre.net

Alex Grimm
011/
www.alexgrimm.com

Álvaro Sanchis
129/
www.alvarosanchis.com

Anna Farré / LILA&TOM
001/
www.quatrevuits.com

Anna Pigem
003/ 009/
www.annapigem.com

Ártico Estudio
147/
www.articoestudio.com

Atelier Flora
126/
judithdrews.de

ATIPUS
017/ 068/ 105/
www.atipus.com

Atosio
132/
www.atosio.com

BAG.Disseny
082/
bagdisseny.com

Barfutura
040/ 056/
www.barfutura.com

Base Design
158/ 159/ 169/
http://www.basedesign.com

BATLLEGROUP
029/
www.batllegroup.com

Beatriz Gimeno Sanz
002/
beatrizgimeno.com

BENBENWORLD
034/ 038/
www.benbenworld.com

Bisgràfic
030/ 084/
bisgrafic.com

Blok Design
054/ 071/ 113/
blokdesign.com

brand attack
167/
www.brandattack.net

Buenaidea - José Fernández Oyarzábal
172/
www.buenaidea.net

Bunch
163/
www.bunchdesign.com

BURO-GDS
015/ 050/
www.buro-gds.com

CADG
115/
cadg.net

Carol García del Busto
055/
www.carolgb.jazztel.es

Cubo Diseño
004/ 090/ 114/
www.cubo.es

Dandelion
036/
dandelionagency.co.uk

David Torrents
023/ 024/ 139/
www.torrents.info

Diseño Cdroig
076/ 110/
www.cdroig.com

Doe de Do
083/
www.doededo.nl

dot.
122/ 125/ 148/
www.dot-info.es

Dúctil
028/ 065/ 135/ 149/
www.ductilct.com

Duo Design
086/
www.duodesign-web.com

Eider Corral Estudio
095/
eidercorral.com

El vivero
060/ 155/
www.elvivero.es

elDiseñador s.c.p
033/
martinezman.com

ENFÁTIKA
109/ 118/ 131/
enfatika.com

Erretres Diseño
106/ 111/
www.erretres.com

extra!
045/ 081/ 091/ 134/
www.extraestudio.com

Fernandez Alvarez®
019/
fernandezalvarez.com

FK Design srl
047/ 057/ 089/
www.fkdesign.it

Fons Hickmann m23
010/ 014/
www.fonshickmann.com

FullblastCreative.com
103/
www.fullblastcreative.com

Gramma
066/
www.gramma.be

GRUPO ANTON COMUNICACIÓN / 6 SOMBREROS CREATIVOS / DISEÑO: FUENSANTA BLANCA
063/
www.grupoanton.es

hazmecaso
074/
http://www.miguelmazon.blogspot.com/

Hoet&Hoet
037/
www.hoet-hoet.eu

Hyperakt
088/ 142/ 143/ 168/
hyperakt.com

Ideario Chinín
112/
chinin.org

Instituto de Gestión de la Información, S.L.
013/
www.visioglobal.com

isebuki / collabor.at
160/
isebuki.com

Jessie Whipple Vickery
173/
www.kunstkraft.com

Juan Martinez Estudio
051/
www.martinezestudio.com

Kanella
018/
www.kanella.com

Keith Kitz
101/
www.onemansstudio.com

Konstantyner Communication & Design
012/
www.konstantyner.dk

La Camorra
043/ 087/
lacamorra.com

Logoorange Design Studio
059/ 062/
www.logoorange.com

Manuel Gracia Gascón
005/
www.carpetademanu.com

Marisa Gallén
079/ 127/
http://www.marisagallen.com

Menta
124/
www.mentagrafica.com

Miller Meiers Design for Communication
121/
www.millermeiers.com

Monsieur Mob
078/
www.monsieurmob.com

Mora Azul Estudio
006/
www.moraazulestudio.com

Murray agencia de diseño
025/ 039/
holamurray.com

MusaWorkLab
016/ 061/ 080/ 094/ 097/
http://www.musaworklab.com

Neil Cutler Design
077/ 085/
www.neilcutler.com

neura projectes, sl
049/
www.neuraprojectes.com

Nifava
007/ 041/ 107/ 117/ 146/ 152/
nifava.com

oikos associati
008/ 058/ 116/
www.oikosassociati.com

Oxigen comunicació gràfica
026/ 108/ 151/
www.oxigen.es

PAPARAJOTE
164/ 166/ 174/
www.paparajote.com

Paragon Marketing Communications
070/ 099/ 133/
www.paragonmc.com

Pau Lamuà
075/ 153/
www.paulamua.com

picnic, ideas surtidas
123/
www.picniccrea.com

poeticsouvenir
145/
www.poeticsouvenir.com

POLIEDRO studio
130/
poliedrostudio.it

projectGRAPHICS
165/
www.projectgraphics.eu

Quattro idcp
102/ 140/ 170/
www.quattroidcp.com

Rafael-Maia
128/
rafael-maia.com

Root Studio
154/
www.rootstudio.co.uk

rumorvisual
022/
www.rumorvisual.com

seesponge
044/
seesponge.com

Signum Comunicación y Diseño, S.L.
093/
www.signum.es

SOGOOD
020/
www.sogooddesign.nl

Sonsoles Llorens
021/ 027/ 031/ 067/ 069/ 098/ 100/
www.sonsoles.com

StudioCentro Marketing srl
104/
www.studiocentromarketing.it

studiosancisi
096/ 138/ 161/ 162/ 175/
studiosancisi.it

Sublima Comunicación
119/
www.sublimacomunica.com

THIS IS Studio
171/
thisisstudio.co.uk

Thonik
120/ 144/
www.thonik.nl

Toormix
048/
www.toormix.com

University of Baltimore
141/
ubalt.edu

Villuendas+Gómez Disseny
032/ 136/ 137/
www.villuendasgomez.com

VIS-TEK
092/ 156/ 157/
www.vis-tek.com

Whitenoise Design Limited
035/ 042/ 046/ 072/
www.whitenoisestudios.com

Xavier Lanau
150/
www.xavierlanau.com

Xavier Martínez Balet
052/
www.xaviermartinez.net